Advance Praise for *Called On*

"*Called On* may be this generation's *One L*, narrating the modern law school experience with all its stress, cut-throat competitiveness, inflated egos, flaws, and triumphs. Early on, the main character observes, 'From what I hear, law school is full of surprises.' Author Lisa McElroy turns that into an understatement, with plot twists that make *Called On* a true page-turner. Anyone who has been to law school, teaches there, or knows lawyers will instantly recognize one or more of McElroy's vivid characters."

— Tony Mauro, Supreme Court Correspondent for *The National Law Journal*

"Lisa McElroy nails law school—from first-day jitters to gunners and back-benchers—in a funny, perceptive, and poignant (but never predictable) first novel. Grab a Diet Coke and a handful of M&Ms and settle in; once you start reading, you won't want to stop."

— Amy Howe, co-founder and editor of SCOTUSblog

"*Called On* is *Legally Blonde*—kicked up a notch. This hilarious first novel follows the heroine through the first year of law school and her encounters with law, justice, first love, and loss. Set aside a rainy weekend to devour this fun read, perfect for fans of Jennifer Weiner and Elin Hildenbrand."

— Paula Froelich, Yahoo Travel Editor-in Chief and host of A Broad Abroad; *New York Times* bestselling author of *Mercury in Retrograde* and former deputy editor of the *New York Post*'s "Page Six"

"Lisa McElroy has provided us with a fresh and modern take on life in law school. The story is told through the eyes of an idealist, who enters law school with the best of intentions only to find that law can be as messy as love. This book is a must read for anyone thinking about taking the plunge into law school."
— Shon Hopwood, author of *Law Man: My Story of Robbing Banks, Winning Supreme Court Cases, and Finding Redemption*

"I didn't go to law school, but author Lisa McElroy did, and that's a great thing for readers of fiction. McElroy uses her personal experience as both a law student and law professor to create a world of high stakes studies, complex personal relationships, and meaningful discussions of themes like liberty and justice. *Called On* is a complete first novel, expertly conceived and skillfully written. Memorable, vivid, and true—the story of two women, one student and one prof, who find themselves in the law."
— Lian Dolan, bestselling author of *Helen of Pasadena* and *Elizabeth the First Wife*

Called On

Called On

Lisa McElroy

QUID PRO BOOKS

New Orleans, Louisiana

Published in 2015 by Quid Pro Books.

ISBN 978-1-61027-326-8 (pbk.)
ISBN 978-1-61027-325-1 (hbk.)
ISBN 978-1-61027-324-4 (ebk.)

QUID PRO BOOKS
Quid Pro, LLC
5860 Citrus Blvd., Suite D-101
New Orleans, Louisiana 70123
www.quidprobooks.com

qp

Publisher's Cataloging-in-Publication

McElroy, Lisa.
    Called on / Lisa McElroy.
        p. cm.
        1. Law schools—Fiction. 2. Law students—Fiction. 3. Law teachers—Fiction. 4. Rhode Island—Fiction. I. Title.
PS3565 .S33 M4 2015

Cover design © 2015 by Alchemy Book Covers and Design.
Interior design © 2015 by QA Productions.

For Zoe and Abby, who bring me more
joy than they will ever know.

For Steve, who is my partner in all things.

For my law students, who inspire me every day.

For Sandra Day O'Connor, who first smiled at me
one day in 1998, instilling in me a great love for justice, a better understanding of the law, and a true
passion for the United States Supreme Court.

In loving memory of the Killer Bs and
Thurgood Tucker McElroy.

Call on (/kɔːl /ɔn, ɑn/); verb

To ask a student a question. In law school, being "called on" by a law professor is a rite of passage, feared by most first-year law students. By the third year of law school, many students simply roll their eyes when a professor calls on them.

Related terms:

Called (/kɔːld/); verb

To feel the need to serve, usually in some type of helpful role. Members of the clergy, people in the medical field, and first responders often describe feeling "called" to their professions.

Called on the carpet (/kɔːld /ɔn, ɑn/ /THə/ˈkɑːrpɪt/); idiom

To be confronted with something one has done wrong, usually by a person in a position of authority.

One

All around Libby, down on the Newport harbor, people were spread out on picnic blankets. Riding beach cruisers. Flip flopping along the sidewalk trying to lap up drips of ice cream with their tongues before the salted caramel or mint chocolate chip or moose tracks turned into sweet, milky soup.

Happy. Everyone was happy. Grinning, even. Loving every second.

Libby pulled her hat down over her face and hurried along the sidewalk, looking down at the pavement, kicking a frisbee and then a melting piece of fudge out of her way.

Bluebird days — where the sun shone bright, the humidity was low, and the sky was that perfect blue little kids paint at preschool easels, their giant smocks almost covering their brushes — bluebird days were a win in nature's lottery for everyone. Everyone but Libby.

Especially in early fall. In the fall, bluebird days were . . . for the birds. In fact, Libby decided as she headed to her apartment to get started with her new project, let the birds have the sunshine, the bright sky, the laughter in the air. Because, this fall, Libby thought, *this* fall she was going to get started on making her own kind of perfection.

Bring it on.

TWO

It had all started when she'd first visited the Supreme Court with her dad and seen Justice O'Connor walking down the hall, wearing a bright purple jacket and looking mighty official. Libby had been eight years old, sure. But that was when she'd discovered what really got her going. From that first iconic sighting on — the cowgirl Justice had even smiled at her! — she'd been a Supreme Court addict. Crunching on popcorn, eating M & M's by the handful, and listening to recorded audio from a Supreme Court argument — now, that was an afternoon for the record books.

It didn't matter to Libby that everyone thought she was crazy. A great snacking regimen, plus visions of Justice O'Connor sponsoring her for the Supreme Court bar someday (hey, a girl could dream, couldn't she?), had inspired her, motivated her, gotten her blood running, for fifteen years. All the way here.

Her resolve had only strengthened the fall she'd turned ten, when she'd looked up at the sky and made the promise to her mother to do her proud.

Unlike at her alma mater, the satellite campus of the state

university she'd called home for four years of undergrad, the class-room doors here were ornate, heavily scrolled wood with bronze handles. She really had to put her weight into pulling one open. Suddenly, 112 pounds seemed even scrawnier than usual.

How was it that she'd suddenly gone weak? Nothing good ever happened when Libby didn't use her muscles. Law school was going to make her mentally tough, emotionally strong. Even if she was physically a barely five-foot-tall shrimp. It was like her mother had always said — brains beat out brawn, every time.

Behind her, a guy in a Harvard T-shirt and a dirty baseball cap reached around her and grabbed the door, even as he looked over his shoulder at a guy absorbed in his phone. "Hey, dude, let's go!" he called. "Back row! No way I'm getting called on the very first day."

Seriously? A Harvard T-shirt? How predictable. Libby looked down at her own baggy "Just Say *Roe!*" shirt and smiled. It was getting kind of ratty. Wearing a shirt twice a week would do that.

Libby shuddered. Getting called on the very first day of law school was a big fear for her, too, one among the many others that had led her here. She'd read the assignment, over and over again, after she'd gotten back to her apartment the night before, well into the morning. Put her under the gun, though, and she'd probably crack. As much as she wanted to emulate Justice O'Connor's cool or Justice Ginsburg's persistence or even Justice Sotomayor's triumph over adversity, she was afraid that she wasn't cut out for this. Her father had told her last night that she was putting too much pressure on herself ("Honey, even Sandra Day O'Connor had a first day of law school"). But this meant something to Libby. If she could get through this first day, and then the day after that, and the day after that . . . then maybe, just maybe, she could actually do Justice O'Connor's legacy proud. And make her smile again. That would be a total wow.

Not to mention the fact that her mom would know, somehow, that Libby had followed in her footsteps. Sort of. In her own, no guts and gore kind of way. Glory, though. Definitely glory.

Here went nothing. Just after a youngish woman who had her arms way too full — so full that Libby had to clear out of the way in case a pile of books and a Diet Coke got dropped on her foot — Libby followed Harvard Boy through the door, holding her cup of coffee tight against her chest. She looked around. Harvard Boy was heading for the back row of seats, trying to grab one before they filled up. The room — one that looked like a courtroom, actually, with its old mahogany moldings and dusty chandeliers — was full of chattering students with heavy casebooks in front of them. There was only one seat left.

Front and center. Great.

Libby twisted her hair around her finger. Should she leave now? Beg a seat in the back from Harvard Boy? Sit on the floor?

Nope. She was a law student now. That took guts, and pride, and forbearance. And no pessimistic attitude. All she had to do was sit down, plug in her laptop, open her casebook, and start taking notes.

Libby was working on having those guts, multiplied exponentially. She wasn't going to let the events of the last several years take her down. Besides, what were the chances that she'd be the very first one asked to stand and recite, out of this entire room of people? And so what if she was? God knew she'd dealt with worse.

•   •   •

Connie Shun finished updating her Facebook status, then pressed "Post."

I've been in school for all but six years of my life: the first three and the three between law school graduation and my first day of teaching at Warren Law. That makes thirty-two first days of school. And I am still nervous, every year.

Connie re-read her post, then shrugged her shoulders. It was true.

Every single year, she wondered what outfit she should wear. The problem this year? James, her best friend since she was practically a child, was not here to give his Queer Eye for the Straight Prof stamp of approval. She hoped the Nanette Lepore suit she'd bought at the consignment shop last week gave off the right vibe. Professional, but not too stuffy. Pretty, but not too attractive. Damn, it was hard being a woman who had to dress in business-not-too-casual for work.

Connie hefted the load of stuff she'd left on the guest chair in her office. Laptop — check. 100 syllabi — check. Casebook that's way too big considering no student ever reads the damn thing — check. Soon-to-be-filled-in seating chart that's ridiculous because the students fight each other for back bench — check. Attendance sheet because the American Bar Association requires it even though no student actually believes she'll fail the class if she doesn't show up — check. Diet Coke — need more than one, but only got one here in the office — check.

It was time to start the semester.

Some of Connie's colleagues — all right, call that most — were seriously moaning in the hallways of the faculty suite that their summers of writing about the application of Proust's *The Search for Lost Time* to AEDPA tolling provisions and the like were over. Now they'd have to teach three hours a week in addition to thinking great thoughts. The indignity of it all was compromising the future of legal scholarship. They sounded like a bunch of cows. In a field. Full of manure.

But Connie secretly thought that her three hours in front of a class of eager minds — even if that was only one or two of them — were the best part of her week. Secretly, mind you, because she'd be dismissed as a serious scholar if she dared admit that anywhere near the faculty lounge. She even liked — gasp! — office hours, if only because those youthful minds came up with the most unlikely questions. "But I don't get it, Professor. Why don't Supreme Court justices have to explain their recusal decisions?" Actually, pretty good questions at that.

Curtain time. Connie hoisted her pile a little higher, clenched a pen in her teeth, and used her elbow to open her office door. In the hallway, standing near the coffee machine, one of her colleagues looked at her in disdain. "Connie, seriously? Don't you think you're taking this class thing a little bit far?"

Connie exited the faculty suite by the admin cubes and headed across the hall to the large lecture room. A young woman with a rolling laptop bag and a terrified look on her face jumped to the side. A guy in a Harvard T-shirt ignored her completely and strode through the heavy door of Connie's classroom, not even holding it for her — actually, not even noticing her. Another guy — this one in jeans and loafers — rushed to grab the door before it hit Connie in the back. Connie smiled at him. The semester had begun. And smiling at these . . . not kids, *students* . . . was the only way to get through.

•   •   •

Libby squeezed into the empty seat. She set her coffee cup down carefully, tossed her casebook down with a thud, stuck her rolling bag under the table, and pulled out her laptop. The woman beside her was taking up all the electrical outlets in the console thing that flipped up from the desk. Did she really need a laptop *and* an iPad *and* what looked like some kind of digital recorder? Libby leaned over and gave her a little wave.

"Hey! Think I could plug in here?"

The woman didn't look up from the — spreadsheet? huh? — she was creating. It looked like a study schedule, with a 16-hour day broken down into six-minute increments.

"Um, hi. I'm Libby. Just wanted to plug in my laptop? Looks like we're in for a long hour or so."

The woman pushed her glasses up on her head.

"Sorry. Need the plugs. Taping and typing, that's my technique. Law review. Order of the Coif. Supreme Court clerkship. Every little bit helps. Early bird gets the worm and all that."

Libby laughed. This woman couldn't be serious. Law school was about saving the northern spotted owl (OK, so Libby was about two decades late for that one), standing up for marriage equality (and about a year late for that one, at least in part), and fighting for equal pay for women (never too late). Plus, the biggie, the terrifying but motivating personal reason Libby had decided to become a lawyer.

Libby shook her head. She wasn't going to think about that right now. But what was this woman talking about? Order of the Coif? Was that some kind of secret society? Never mind, Libby thought. She didn't actually want to know.

"Yeah, I know, right? But can't do it without plugging in." Libby decided to go along to get along. Plus get an outlet.

The woman stared. "I *am* plugged in."

Libby didn't want to lose her cool. But seriously?

"Yeah, so, don't you think it's fair for us all to be on the same playing field?"

The woman put her glasses back on her nose. "We are. We can all get here early. And use the plugs we need. And those who don't should just realize that they aren't cut out to be federal appeals court judges."

Libby looked around for another outlet, bumping her laptop and knocking over her coffee in the process. She watched helplessly as it puddled on the floor near the podium. Her hands just wouldn't stop shaking, which pissed Libby off. She hated letting people see when she was scared. Plus, so much for making friends, let alone making a difference.

Justice for all. Yeah, right. And now her "Just Say *Roe!*" T-shirt looked like a baby northern spotted owl had crapped all over it. Libby reached into her bag for a sweatshirt. Thank God for Chief Justice John Marshall, the epic chief from the early 19th century — this giant WWJD ("What Would John Do") hoodie would keep Libby from looking like she was entering a wet T-shirt contest instead of what was turning out to be a "claw your way to the top" law school version of *The Hunger Games*.

All righty, then. All set. Except that Libby wasn't sure what to do about the coffee. Should she call the janitor? She looked around the room to see whether anyone might come to her aid with a stack of paper towels or something, but then she got distracted by the look Madam Future Justice of the Supreme Court was giving her. Jesus. The woman seemed to be writing down something about negligence and liability for coffee burns. What did she think Libby was, McDonald's? Libby never even had enough extra money to eat there very often, much less run the mega-corporation. Which Libby was against. Of course. Because they put chicken beaks in their nuggets and exploited their workers.

OK, Libby. Practice what you've learned. Locate your center. Find the zone.

Listen to the podium crash . . .

Oh, crap.

Three

All of the chatter in the room stopped and gaped. Harvard Boy cackled and pointed. The guy in the loafers gasped, then stood. Even the spreadsheet-loving plug hoarder looked up.

Someone who looked an awful lot like a law professor was lying on the floor in the front of the room, near the collapsed podium, in a pool of coffee.

Libby had to give the woman credit — that had been one heck of a graceful fall, one Libby couldn't have managed. The casebook was lying about ten feet away, it was true, and a bunch of papers were still floating towards the floor in sort of a Fellini-esque montage. But *damn*. That professor — if a professor she was — had her priorities straight. Her skirt still covered her knees, her laptop laid on top of her chest, and her right hand clutched a 20-ounce bottle of Diet Coke. If Justice O'Connor had fallen in a pool of coffee, this is how she'd look. Together. In the least together situation ever.

Libby had never once in her life been that graceful. Not even when she took ballet for about a month as a six-year-old. (Yes, she had won the coveted role of a purple rock in the end-of-class recital. Don't ask.)

But she startled back to the present when the future jurist beside her smirked, poked her in the side, and said, "Nice work. First day of law school, and you take the professor out."

Libby gripped the desk, closed her eyes, and asked herself, "WWJD?"

There, in her front row center seat, Libby had an unobstructed view of the look of horror on the probably-the-professor's face. And the coffee — pretty recently hot coffee — that was all over her fashionable (at least as far as Libby could tell) skirt and jacket.

This whole law school thing was not starting off so well.

•   •   •

A way over-teched and over-groomed woman in the front row jumped up and pushed her way past everyone else at the long lecture hall table. She rounded the corner to the podium.

"Ma'am, can I help you up?" She grabbed the hand that wasn't gripping the Diet Coke.

Connie pushed her way up into a stand. Coffee dripped onto the floor. From her skirt. And her jacket. And her hair.

At least her blouse was safely buttoned under the jacket.

"Keep your sense of humor, Connie," she muttered to herself. "They're 1Ls. This is their first day. Don't go all Professor Kingsfield on them."

A crowd of students now surrounded her. Great. They'd probably see the giant zit on her chin. Connie had been counting on the fact that it wouldn't be visible from the podium.

Connie accepted a pile of napkins from the student in the loafers. He looked like he'd hit Starbucks — and swiped an entire container of napkins — before arriving at class. She mopped at her hair and patted her skirt.

Good enough. Another student had grabbed the casebook and her papers. And she didn't really need her notes for this class, anyway.

She could teach this in her sleep.

Connie motioned the students back to their seats. She was fine, she pantomimed with a tight smile. She had it together. No matter that she was completely flustered. If she could just get them back where they belonged, up in the gallery, they wouldn't be able to tell. And if they couldn't tell, she'd be able to get back into her groove.

Connie arranged her stuff just so on a table, plugged in her laptop, took a deep breath, and looked out at the room. Now, then.

"So," Connie began. "Let's see who's here." She looked out at the table-tented name tags the students had placed in front of their seats.

"Thanks to Mr. . . . Matthews? . . . for the napkins."

The guy with the loafers nodded and grinned.

"And to Ms. . . . Jackson? . . . for rescuing my stuff."

An African-American woman with cornrows smiled just a little bit.

"Ms. . . . Everly? Thanks for the hand. I'm fine. No EMT needed." Connie paused.

"But, well, it wouldn't be right to start class without thanking Ms. . . . Behl for the entertainment, right? Nice move with the coffee.

"Ms. Behl?"

Connie glanced down at her attendance sheet, did a tiny double take, then made eye contact with the student who had spilled the coffee. Should she out this kid — *student* — on the very first day?

What the heck. It would make it even more memorable.

"Ms. *Liberty* Behl?"

The class erupted into laughter. A preppy guy in the back row (wearing a Harvard T-shirt, naturally — that type always flaunted it) hooted. The teched-out woman — Ms. Everly, apparently — in the front row stared at Ms. Behl in disbelief. Mr. Matthews and Ms. Jackson giggled.

"It's so nice to meet you, Ms. Behl. Welcome to Warren Law. Maybe you can start us off? We've got some fascinating material to cover today."

Connie ignored Ms. Behl's red face and shaking hands. Someone had to go first. In other years, she'd probably have picked the trying-to-be-suave Harvard guy. He had that cocky attitude that she liked to challenge. But when a student made her do a slip and slide in coffee? Before they even got started? Yeah, this one was a no-brainer. Ms. Liberty Behl would get called on first. And she'd probably remember it for the rest of her life.

Connie still remembered who'd gotten called on first in her law school class. It had been her friend Sarah. Sarah had held her own, though, and she still did. She was rising through the ranks faster than Connie had slid across the room just now.

No, getting called on first never hurt anybody.

Connie settled herself on the edge of the desk at the front of the room, holding a slide show clicker. She was actually — honestly — glad the podium was toast, even if that meant she couldn't hide behind it. She'd always felt sort of like a fraud standing behind that podium, anyway, especially since the day her TA had reported to her that no one believed her when she told the class she'd been teaching for eight years. They were pretty sure she'd been born about eleven years ago. Being short and blond could do that to a girl. In law school, all the guys with the smooth haircuts and Tag Heuer watches had assumed she was some kind of Southern cheerleader. Until she opened her mouth. Yeah, that usually threw them for a loop.

She tilted her bottle of Diet Coke back, took a swig, and looked at the class.

"OK, Ms. Behl, so I'll bet you're interested in doing justice, right?"

The look on the student's face was wary. She probably wasn't sure whether this was a trick question. Things hadn't been going so well for the kid — the *student* — so far.

But Connie had to give Ms. Behl credit. The student squared her shoulders and met Connie's eye.

"Yes. That's why I came to law school. I'm interested in helping people. I guess I sort of feel . . . called."

The Harvard T-shirt clown in the back row rolled his eyes and elbowed the guy sitting next to him.

"Great," Connie continued. "So I'd like to tell you a story. It's about the Olympics."

It was pretty obvious that she'd thrown Ms. Behl for a loop. The students were always confused when Connie started talking about sports. Wasn't this a law school class? Connie smiled as she looked out over the classroom at the group of students. She loved that puzzled look most of them had. Confusion mixed with intrigue was exactly what she was going for. Sure, that woman next to Ms. Behl with about thirty-two electronic devices plugged in — she was going to be a hard sell — but Ms. Behl looked like the type who would get with the program. Connie just had to reel her in.

"You know," Connie explained, "you're probably confused about why the heck I'm talking about the Olympics. This is law school, right? But sports are actually a really good metaphor for how justice works. And how law works. So, Ms. Behl, are those the same thing?"

"Law and justice?"

Connie nodded.

"Well, yeah. The purpose of the law is to do what's fair . . . it's to make things right."

"OK, then. So think about this example.

"The Summer Games of 2004 — you were in junior high then, right? — were in Athens. Like it usually is, gymnastics was one of the biggest draws. Everyone likes gymnastics. Right? Mr. . . . . Kraft?" Boy, those table tents came in handy when she wanted to call someone out.

Harvard Boy looked up from his iPhone with a smirk. "Of course, Professor Shun. Naturally."

"So, Mr. Kraft, you undoubtedly know that, in the men's all-around gymnastics competition, Paul Hamm was heavily favored to win gold. You remember him, right? He was a petite guy? Big muscles?"

"Right. Absolutely." Kraft kicked his buddy under the table. Connie watched as he whispered to his comrade. Kraft was probably asking "Was this in the reading, man?" Nope. It hadn't been. But Connie figured she was throwing Kraft off balance. Good.

"Well, for those of you who aren't huge gymnastics fans like Mr. Kraft, here's a photo." Connie clicked the remote in her hand. An image of a buff, freckled redhead on a pommel horse filled the screen.

"Paul Hamm did win gold in the summer of 2004.

"Or did he? Lots of people think he didn't, at least according to the spirit of the sport.

"Because he had a worthy opponent: Yang Tae-Young. Koreans' last names come first — right, Mr. Kraft? — so we'll call him 'Yang.' "

Connie clicked again. An image of a tall Asian man swinging his way through the parallel bars dropped in next to the photo of the redhead.

"Yang was a South Korean superstar, and he would have scored higher than Paul Hamm, except that the judges made a scoring error. Because the judges messed up, Yang ended up with the bronze medal.

"What do you think, Ms. Behl? Was that fair?"

The student shook her head. "No, Professor Shun. That was not fair. The Olympics are all about letting the best athlete win!"

"Mr. Kraft?"

"Um . . . I'm gonna go with yes?" The room laughed. The students were starting to relax, Connie could tell, but they still had their guard up. They should, she thought. They had no idea where this was going.

Connie watched as Kraft wrote a note to his buddy. It always amazed her that the students thought she couldn't see them. Well, she'd keep Kraft on the hook.

"All right," said Connie. "We've got a real debate going on here. And back in 2004, there was a worldwide debate. Who was right? What was fair? Who should win?"

Connie clicked again. A new slide appeared, this time with a complicated set of scoring rules.

"In 2004, as gymnastics was then scored, a '10' was the highest possible 'start value.' Essentially, that meant that the harder a gymnast's routine, the higher the score he could potentially earn. But, as you can see from the slide, the rules also said that any scoring dispute had to be raised before a gymnast moved on to the next apparatus. You've all seen this, right? When they move to the next apparatus?"

Connie walked across the front of the room, her head high, shoulders back, toes pointed. The class laughed again.

"Right? So, like, when the gymnasts complete a parallel bars routine, that's one apparatus. So before they can move on to the pommel horse or the vault or whatever, they have to either protest their scores or forever hold their peace."

Connie clicked to show photos of the parallel bars and the pommel horse.

"So here's what happened. Yang's parallel bars routine was super challenging, and the judges should have given him a start value of 10. They made a mistake, though, and scored his routine out of 9.9. That might seem like a small mistake, but in gymnastics, every tenth of a point counts. In fact, in Yang's case, the tenth mattered so much that when the final all-around scores were calculated, Yang had won the bronze medal, not the gold as he would have if the judges had scored the routine correctly. Hamm had won the gold.

"Everybody with me?"

The class nodded. The techie woman in the front row typed frantically. Ms. Behl gave the typing maniac a blank stare that seemed to say, "What the hell could she be writing about? The professor hasn't even gotten to the point yet."

No, Connie hadn't gotten to the point. But she was about to. She loved this part.

"So, after the competition, all officials — including the competition judges, FIG (that's the Federation of International Gymnastics), and the U.S. Olympics Committee — agreed that the scoring had been wrong and that Yang should have won over Hamm and the silver medalist.

"So, Ms. Behl, what do you think the problem was?"

The student's face reflected that she was deep in thought. Then she appeared to make up her mind that she'd take a stab at it. Connie didn't mind if the student took a minute. Better that than spewing out some nonsense just to say something.

"I'm thinking that Yang and his coaches didn't protest until after he moved on to the next apparatus?"

Connie beamed. This Liberty Behl might have gotten off on the wrong foot, but she could rally. That was Connie's favorite kind of student.

"Yes!" Connie cheered. "In fact, Yang did not protest until sometime around the medal ceremony. So, Mr. Kraft, what does that mean?"

"Hamm got the gold because of a technicality, not because he was the best gymnast." At this point, it appeared that Kraft's seatmate had looked it up on Google, because Kraft was looking super-confident. Connie smiled to herself. That was OK. Kraft was going to find out pretty quickly that the Internet was unlikely to help him in this class, most of the time. But at least for now, Kraft seemed to know where she was going with this.

"So, Ms. Behl, what do you think? Justice?"

The student closed her eyes, opened them, and dug in deep. "No, not justice. The best athlete should win. This is the Olympics we're talking about! It's only every four years! Yang's probably never going to get another chance!"

"Mr. Kraft?"

"Well, I mean, there have to be rules, right?"

Connie smiled. Suddenly, the class had become like a tennis match. The dozens of students in the room were looking up and down, up and down, from Kraft to Behl and back. Epic rally. Bingo.

"You're both onto something. Practically as soon as the medal ceremony was over, there was an outcry across the world. Koreans, Americans, and the FIG called for Hamm to give up his gold to Yang voluntarily, saying that the Olympics were about sportsmanship and that a good sport would recognize the true winner. Hamm refused, though, and the U.S. Olympic Committee backed him up. They argued that sports are about rules, he followed the rules, and so he won fair and square. Hamm was called a bad sport, and Yang was called a Korean national hero. And yet, at the end of the day, Hamm went down in history as a gold medal winner, and Yang did not.

"So, Ms. Behl, what do you think should have happened? Should Wheaties have put Paul Hamm on the box? General Mills refused, by the way."

"I — I'm not sure."

"Mr. Kraft? Should Hamm have gone down in disgrace? Should Yang have gotten the $20,000 that the Korean Olympic Committee eventually awarded him, saying that he really did win the gold? Why?"

"But — but he didn't follow the rules." Connie could see that Kraft was looking for the answer on Google. He wasn't finding it.

"A tip, Mr. Kraft," Connie said, looking at him hard from her seat on the table. "This is law school. OK, so it doesn't seem like it because we're talking about gymnastics, but, hey, I'm easing you in here.

"In law school, the answers just aren't going to be Googleable. If they were, your clients wouldn't need you. So put down the phone and close the laptop and think through the problem."

Kraft laughed nervously, then looked around the room. This first day of law school thing wasn't going quite like he'd expected, either. He stuck out his Harvard-emblazoned chest, to catch her eye, Connie assumed.

Connie ignored him and continued. "So what do you think, Ms. Behl? Sounds like you think that the rule about the timing of protests should have been waived here? Because there was a really clear error?"

"Yes, I do." The student was getting more confident. "It wasn't like there was any question. Yang scored higher than Hamm. Should he really lose out on the gold medal because the judges messed up? That seems so wrong to me."

"Mr. Kraft? Do you think it would have worked to waive the rule this one time? Is Ms. Behl right that Yang shouldn't have been penalized for the judges' mistake?"

"Well . . ." Kraft paused. He was still sort of floored that he couldn't look up the answers. "If they waived it this time, wouldn't that be a problem for next time?"

Connie did a secret fist pump in her head. "So, what you're saying, Mr. Kraft, is that changing the rule this time would establish bad precedent? And the decision about whether to waive the rules would become a sort of slippery slope?"

Tech Woman typed. Precedent . . . slippery slope — or so Connie guessed.

"Well, no," Ms. Behl cut in. "Because you could limit it to times when the judges clearly screwed up. Like Justice Powell said he did when he joined the Supreme Court's opinion against sodomy. Although that was about a different kind of screwing."

"Yang screwed up, too!" Kraft yelled. "He should have protested in time. So, what, would we let him protest a year later, if he finally figured it out then?"

Connie waited a beat to let Kraft's idea sink in.

"Ms. Behl?"

"But the best gymnast in the world came in third! How is that right?"

"Because you need rules in sports! Otherwise you have, I don't know, anarchy! How could anyone ever play?" Kraft was rising up in his seat.

His buddy put his hand on Kraft's shoulder and pushed him down. "Dude! Chill!"

"But how is that fair? Yang lost the thing he'd worked for his whole life!"

"Because the fairest way to go is to be consistent. You gotta deal when sometimes that doesn't work out the way you want!"

Connie sat and watched. For all the crap law school had been taking in the media lately, this was the kind of class discussion that proved all the "law school is a scam" bloggers wrong. She didn't have to do anything but get the students started with a provocative question. Then they took over.

She just couldn't understand why her colleagues' blood didn't pump with adrenaline in the classroom.

The class quieted, thinking. Tech Woman typed. Consistent . . . Connie just knew it.

It was time to give them a nudge. "OK, well, Hamm didn't give the medal back. But he didn't get on the Wheaties box, either. So he's got a stain on his gold medal, don't you think? Even though he won it.

"So, you all think this was an isolated incident? Fast forward to June, 2010. Anyone know who this guy is?" She clicked the remote to bring up a photo of a baseball pitcher in a blue and orange cap. "Ms. Behl?"

The student laughed. "No clue. Secretary of State?"

Kraft pumped his fist. "Galarraga! Detroit Tigers!"

"You got it in one, Mr. Kraft. Any thoughts on why he's up here?"

"Because he got robbed of his perfect game!"

"Yep," confirmed Connie. "Want to tell the story? Without Googling?"

"Yeah, I don't think I need to Google this one. So what happened was, Armando Galarraga was living the dream. He was one out away from being, like, the twenty-first pitcher in major league baseball history to throw a perfect game. Perfect games, like, never happen. But then the ump called the last batter 'safe' on first. Everyone was screaming! He was out! The ump totally screwed the call! And they played it back on instant replay, and yeah, the batter was so out."

"So then what happened?" Ms. Behl asked.

"They wouldn't give him the perfect game . . ." Kraft answered, his voice trailing off.

"And why not?" Connie probed.

"Because there was this rule. That said you can't use instant replay to override the ump's call." Kraft looked confused. Hold on a minute. Hadn't he been arguing that rules should always be applied consistently?

Tech Woman started packing up her laptop. She reached over Behl to pull her cords out of the outlet.

Connie gave Tech Woman a look and checked out her table tent. "Ms. . . . Everly? Not so interested in how things turned out?"

"Well, Professor Shun, it's not that! It's just that you seem to be really into rules. And class was supposed to end four minutes ago."

Connie glanced at Ms. Behl. Ms. Behl did a tiny eye roll.

"OK, everyone, then check the class website for the assignment for Wednesday. Introduction to Legal Thinking, Professor Shun. Just a heads up — this assignment will require you to work in groups, so check soon so that you can meet up with your group members. Ciao until then."

Four

Libby figured that now was as good a time as any to check the Intro to Legal Thinking class website. First, though, she really needed coffee. She'd gone an entire hour looking longingly at the leftover puddles near the podium. "WWJD?" She didn't think John Marshall would have lapped them up with his tongue. Even Justice David Souter, who, as legend would have it, brewed one pot of coffee in the morning and then reheated it all day, probably would not resort to puddle slurping.

And dignity mattered to Libby. Sometimes it was all that mattered. That, and honor.

Legal Grounds it was.

They'd probably have plugs in the student coffee shop, right? Her laptop's battery light was blinking red.

Libby dumped her stuff at an empty table near the back. Legal Grounds was hopping; Libby figured that a lot of those beverage-downing, sweatshirt-wearing students had to be 1Ls, given the shocked looks on their faces and the "drop out of law school" forms in their hands.

OK, not really on the forms thing. But pretty much nothing would shock Libby at this point.

Libby joined the line and ponied up $1.30 for a large latte. She'd questioned the price — really? Did the barista understand that she wanted a large? As in, a really, really humungous cup of coffee?

Turned out the law school *subsidized* student coffee purchases. Huh. Maybe the dean was trying to make up for the torture inflicted in the classroom. Nice approach. Anyone who was into nurturing others instead of hurting them was OK with Libby.

Libby booted up her laptop — thank God Everly the Plug Hoarder was nowhere in sight — and logged on to the class website.

There it was. Introduction to Legal Thinking. ILT. Professor Connie T. Shun.

On the home page, Professor Shun had posted a Calvin & Hobbes cartoon. The kid and the tiger were talking about a brand new world after a snowstorm. They were going exploring.

Libby smiled to herself. She actually kind of liked Professor Shun. She *really* liked Calvin & Hobbes. Only thing better? SCOTUSblog. She loved a good underdog story, like a blog that had gone from a tiny law firm enterprise to the authoritative source on all things Supreme Court, all without a press pass. In fact, Libby intended to be an underdog success story herself.

Libby clicked on the left tool bar and pulled up the first assignment.

The law/justice dichotomy we discussed in class today is a tricky thing — if, in fact, it is a dichotomy. As Oliver Wendell Holmes and Judge Learned Hand are reported to have said on the occasion of Holmes's appointment to the United States Supreme Court, "Do justice, sir." "That is not my job. My job is to apply the law." Was Holmes right? Should the law always control? Or was Holmes's view too rigid?

We can apply our understanding of the athletic examples to legal situations in which the law/justice divergence (or intersection, depending on how you look at it) occurs.

To some, these are miscarriages of justice of Olympic proportions. And to some, these decisions are just, because they comply with the law. Can every situation be judged on the equities? Does every legal dispute have two sides? Sometimes, both sides can make good legal arguments, and sometimes both sides can argue that their way of looking at the facts is the just way. Our job as lawyers? It's to ferret out these arguments and apply them on behalf of our clients.

For this assignment, meet with your group and think of an example in which law and justice seem to diverge. In class on Wednesday, I'll ask you to present your ideas to the class.

Let the games begin.

This was pretty cool. Libby could do a lot of WWJD thinking here. Thank God for the great Chief. Maybe this class was where she'd really figure out what her own version of justice was.

Libby raised her paper cup to her lips for a long, satisfying draw as she checked out the groups for the first assignment. And then she choked.

She had been placed in a group with . . . wait for it . . . Kraft and Everly.

Where could she get those withdrawal forms, again?

•   •   •

Anderson Kraft walked straight through the now-upscale fishing town to his grandmother's house and the studio apartment above her garage where he lived. When, much to his disbelief, he'd actually gotten into Warren Law School off the wait list, only a week before school started — how the heck did that happen? — he'd been totally stoked, and not just because WLS was one of the top law schools in the country. No, as corny as it sounded for a twenty-two-year-old guy, he seriously loved spending time with his Nana in her cottage on Newport Harbor. She was smart as a whip and unafraid to tell him exactly what she thought. Given that Anderson worked hard to give people the impression that he was super-confident (not to mention super-suave), Nana's ability to know when he was really struggling to stay afloat was a breath of fresh air, as counterintuitive as that sounded. When he'd been a kid, a week or two of her soft hugs and her trademark "Stand straight and own it, son" had been the best part of his year.

Walking down Spring Street and smelling the salty ocean air, Anderson was kind of . . . well . . . nervous. He was sure that Nana and her coffee with chicory root were exactly what he needed right now. He just didn't know whether he should tell her about how horrendous Intro to Legal Thinking had been today. She definitely wouldn't approve of the fact that he'd been pretty lame in needing Google to hold up his end of the discussion, that was for sure.

He had never realized that the prof might ask about random, non-legal stuff. Honestly, it wasn't really fair that Professor Shun had done that. If she wanted to call on people, she should do it on the stuff she'd assigned.

What was he supposed to do? Admit that he didn't really get what she was talking about? Not a chance. The only way through law school was at the top of the pack. If other people were intimidated by his apparent smarts, that could only help him, right?

And so he needed to come up with a way to keep Nana from seeing through him today. But even if she did, surely she would see that it really, truly wasn't his fault. Right? Even if the smarts were pretty much a fake.

Nana would say he should never fake. He should get up his gumption, and he should do what he needed to do to make sure he was better prepared next time.

OK. When Nana asked him about the first day, and the first class, and the first questions asked, he was just going to stand up straight and tell her confidently that he'd aced it.

Really? Could he do that? What if he told her the truth? Would Nana say, "No Jell-o mold for you"? Worse, would she put Anderson's favorite blanket in the washing machine? He couldn't stand that. It had to smell a certain way. Like it had when he was five. And it was totally OK that he was now twenty-two and still liked it. People were allowed to like what they liked. And it wasn't like he took it with him to sleepover dates with girls or anything. He was smarter than *that*.

His parents had always tried to take away his favorite blanket as a punishment. And they'd told him that sugar only exacerbated his problems. That was how he'd ended up figuring out that he had to act all confident, all the time. And that was how he'd ended up living with Nana during breaks, starting his freshman year of college. Sure, Nana didn't usually buy his "don't mess with me," but everyone else did. When Nana had agreed to pay for law school (against her better judgment, she'd said) if he kept himself in line, plus sworn never to wash blankie, he'd figured it was his chance to show his parents how totally wrong they'd been about him. He wasn't a sadistic bully. He was a good guy.

Now he was — deep down, nowhere near the surface — seriously worried that they had been right.

As Anderson took the fork onto Farewell Street, he stopped wavering. He was an adult now. He didn't have to tell Nana everything. No, with this law school thing, he was going to make Nana proud, make her admit that paying for law school had been a good gamble. He'd even show his parents that he had the right stuff.

Anderson took off his sweatshirt, wrapped it around his waist, stretched his arms to the sky, and started to whistle. On Poplar, he turned and stepped up his pace. He was almost there. He was only a few blocks from law school, but it was a whole different world down here on the water. Down here, he could sit on the deck, watch the boats, and feel the day slip away.

Anderson walked up the stone path to Nana's front door. It needed paint. He'd have to haul out a brush and a gallon of periwinkle blue this weekend. He smiled thinking of how Nana's face would light up when she saw the color of the ocean newly reflected in her cottage's entryway.

Anderson squared his shoulders and reminded himself, "What she doesn't know won't hurt her." He pulled the cord to ring the old-fashioned nautical bell hanging from the eaves. He waited. And then Nana opened the door and opened her arms to her grandson for a big hug.

•   •   •

Connie collapsed in her office. First class — done. First impression — made. First M & M's of the day — needed.

Like always, Connie wondered how her office got so messy. It was only the first day of the semester. Why were there books stacked in the corner already? Why weren't her papers filed? Why did she even have a filing cabinet, anyway, when pretty much all her documents were electronic nowadays?

Some questions just couldn't be answered. Just like her office would never be organized.

Connie glanced through her email as she pulled a two-pound bag of chocolate heaven from her desk drawer. Where she kept it under a large bag of kale chips.

She smiled when she caught a glimpse of Sarah Abernathy's name in the "From" column.

From: Sarah Abernathy
        <judge_abernathy@rid.uscourts.gov>
To: Connie T. Shun <cshun@warrenlawschool.edu>
Date: September 3, 2014 12:34:19
Re: After work?

Hey, lady,

First day of classes and all. How are those young, fertile minds in ILT?

Want to grab a beer after work? Crimson & Blue? You've been thinking about justice all day. Justice dictates that you down some potato skins and Bud Light. "Light," to offset the potato skins. The perfect combo.

Sarah

Connie popped two M & M's into her mouth and sucked the candy shell off. She typed back.

From: Connie T. Shun <cshun@warrenlawschool.edu>
To: Sarah Abernathy
       <judge_abernathy@rid.uscourts.gov>
Date: September 3, 2014 13:14:42
Re:Re: After work?

OMG, Your Honor, you know it! It was kind of a crazy first class — I'll fill you in when I see you. For now, let's just put it like this: I have to go home now and change before I walk Felix.

I've had nothing but kale chips to eat all day, so those potato skins will hit the spot.

Okay, girlfriend. Gotta get stuff together. I'll meet you at C & B at around 6ish. I'll be the one with a paper bag over her head in case any of my students are there.

Ciao for now.

Connie

The day was getting better and better.

Connie opened another new email and let autofill put in Sarah's name.

From: Connie T. Shun <cshun@warrenlawschool.edu>
To: Sarah Abernathy
          <judge_abernathy@rid.uscourts.gov>
Date: September 3, 2014 13:17:26
Re:Re:Re: After work?

   BTW, I have a really intriguing new student. I'll tell you more at
   C & B. I think this one has some real potential.

Two more M & M's. So mmmmm. The name was genius.
Connie's email pinged.

From: Sarah Abernathy
          <judge_abernathy@rid.uscourts.gov>
To: Connie T. Shun <cshun@warrenlawschool.edu>
Date: September 3, 2014 13:18:12
Re:Re:Re:Re: After work?

   Uh huh. Kale chips. Right.

   But I'll go along with the no-chocolate-comfort fiction if that
   makes you feel more virtuous.

   Just don't let Felix Frankfurter eat any. Chocolate is toxic for
   dachshunds.

   See you 'round 6!

   Sarah

   P.S. Part of your charm — and your naïvete — is that you think
   they ALL have potential. Can you imagine what would happen
   if I thought that about all the criminal defendants who appeared
   before me? But I know what you mean. Every once in a while,
   one stands out. This one must be really special if you're already
   elevating her above the rest.

Five

Libby walked in through the door of C & B and looked around. It was a familiar scene. Even though things at Warren were mostly very different than they'd been at the big public university she'd attended undergrad, some things never changed. The smell of beer, the clack of pool balls, and the Katy Perry hits on the jukebox were constants of American education and the campus bars that were an integral part of it.

Libby was determined that bars would be just that for her: a place to listen to music, play some pool, and drink some beer. Nothing else. Starting today.

It looked like most of the 1L class had decided to celebrate the end of the first day with a beer. The wooden bar tables were crowded; most students were standing, with all the stools taken.

Sure, *they* could celebrate. *They* hadn't been the first ones called on. *They* didn't hate bars with a vengeance.

Libby scouted the place for Kraft and Everly. She figured they'd be somewhere between the bar and the nearest electrical outlet. Yep. There they were. Right by the wall of photos of famous alums.

"Over here, Libby!" Everly waved a skinny arm. She was awfully dressed up to be at a beer hall, Libby thought. Libby had ditched the coffee-stained T-shirt but kept the WWJD sweatshirt on. Everly, on the other hand, had on a dress. And heels. And lipstick.

"OK, Libby, you don't have to like these people," she said to herself. "You don't have to love this place. You just have to get this assignment done so that you can pass Intro to Legal Thinking. And then you can change the world. Somehow. Instead of just passing through it."

Libby smiled and put her stuff down, and sat down between Kraft and Everly. Everly moved her stool a little closer to Kraft. "Just making sure my cord doesn't come unplugged!" she said brightly.

Kraft stood up and pulled out Libby's stool. "Quinn got here first and found the only plug in the place, so she has offered to be our scribe for this session. But, first, Libby, a drink for you? A snack?" Kraft smiled.

Libby sat down, then wobbled as Kraft pushed the stool in for her. She straightened up.

"Um, I don't know, how about a Diet Coke?" she asked.

"You've got to be kidding, Libby! We made it through our first day of law school!" Kraft answered. "Live it up!"

"You know what? You're right. Can you ask them to add a shot of rum?"

"Now you're talking. Be right back." Kraft picked up his own empty glass and headed to the bar.

"So, Quinn. It's Quinn, right?" Libby turned toward the third member of the group.

Quinn nodded, then took a sip of a pink drink in a slanted glass. It smelled like gin. Libby hated gin.

"Good day?" Libby asked.

"It was fine. I took a lot of notes. I noticed you don't take many. In Law Stars, they really emphasized that notetaking is critical. What your professor says and thinks is the key to rising above the pack." Quinn looked down at her computer and opened a new document.

Just based on what she'd seen, Libby thought it was the fifth or sixth one Quinn had started that day.

"Well," Libby answered. She wondered if Kraft would be back with her rum and Diet Coke soon. "I guess I'm lucky Shun put me in your group, then!"

"Right. You totally are. And I'm so glad she put me in with Kraft. He went to Harvard. He's like our generation's Ted Cruz, who would only study with top Ivy grads when he was at Harvard Law. That's how I'm planning to form my study group. Only way to the top."

"Sure thing," answered Libby. Ivy grads who drank Pink Ladies. Libby's kind of crowd. Not so much.

"And . . . for you, Libby Behl! Rum and Diet Coke! The Olympic champion of drinks!" Kraft did a little twirl with his hand as he put it in front of her.

Libby glanced at Quinn. She was looking down at her study spreadsheet and pretending not to notice the fact that Kraft was sort of . . . flirting? with Libby.

Libby was sure she must have that wrong. Kraft was totally not her type. Ugh. The very thought. Even if Libby wasn't sure what she was into, she knew it wasn't misogynists. Quinn could have them.

This called for a drink. Libby took a big gulp and wiped her mouth on her sweatshirt.

"Wow, that hits the spot," Libby said.

Kraft looked surprised. "Wow. Wouldn't have figured you'd be a drinking kind of girl," he said.

Quinn blanched.

Libby shrugged. "From what I hear, law school is full of surprises." She took another swig and crunched the ice. "So, should we get to work?"

•   •   •

"Hey, girl!" Connie shouted across the bar. "I'm over here!" She waved at Sarah, who was wobbling her way through the open door on spike-heeled boots.

Sarah started weaving her way through the student crowd.

"Where are you?"

Connie was in a booth in the back, hiding behind a menu. She'd just spotted Kraft, Everly, and Behl at a table near the bar. Great. Just what she needed. Now she couldn't even dance on tables. Not that she would. But still. She couldn't. She hated it when her liberty was limited.

"What are you doing? You look like Felix Frankfurter after he's eaten cat poop in the bushes." Sarah pushed her way into the other side of the booth. She took off her lace sweater and fluffed her hair.

"Thanks, friend. Just what I needed to hear." Connie frowned and tilted her head toward the bar. "A bunch of my new students are over there. I knew we should have chosen a different spot."

"Hey, look, does it hurt for them to see you as human?" Sarah asked. "I mean, I'm always trying to convince the parties who appear before me that I'm human, just like they are. Putting on a black robe a couple of times a week doesn't change my essence."

"I don't know. I really don't. I feel like I really struggle with that. I mean, remember when James died? And I had to miss work for several days? I told my students that I had had a 'family' emergency," Connie made air quotes with her fingers, "but I didn't tell them what had happened.

"But then I got emails from several of them asking whether there was any chance we could have our review session anyway. They were just too anxious about the exam to reschedule. Well, you know what? I was anxious, too. Those emails made me so upset. And I didn't feel like I could explain myself. When your best friend dies, are students really supposed to care?"

Sarah sat there looking at Connie, a bemused smile on her face.

"You know what, sister? You are way too serious for a night out on the town. Now, I'm going to order you a rum and Diet Coke and make sure the potato skins are on their way."

"Christ. OK. Just help me make small talk if they stop by our table."

"No problem. And they won't. Their law prof is the last person they want to see tonight." Sarah went up to the bar to order.

Ms. Behl got up and headed across the bar in the direction of the bathroom. She caught Connie's eye. Connie smiled. The student smiled back. Then the student continued to the restroom.

Connie breathed. Not only was that kid — *student* — smart, she had common sense.

Sarah came back with the drinks. "To having fun!"

"Even if students are sitting nearby." Connie raised her glass and drank. "To my favorite drink and my favorite friend."

•   •   •

Libby took the last sip of her drink. Sometime around 8:00, she'd switched to virgin Diet Coke, all the better to figure this assignment out, plus keep her wits about her. "OK, so we're done, then? Quinn, you'll hand in our assignment in the electronic dropbox?"

"Done. Just got the email confirming that the system received it." Quinn closed the laptop and reached behind her to unplug. "You think every night of law school is going to be like this? Working until 11:00 p.m. and not even getting all of the reading done?"

"From what I hear, it only sucks more from here," Kraft groaned.

Libby pulled her roller bag out from under the table. "All I know is, it could be worse. We had caffeine, and the assignment was seriously interesting. Did you check out that Civil Procedure reading? It's all about something called subject matter jurisdiction."

Kraft perked up. "You read Civ Pro already?"

Libby shrugged. "Yeah, I figured if we were meeting tonight, I'd better get it out of the way."

Quinn looked at Libby, a frown on her face. "But you didn't take notes on it, right?"

Libby didn't know whether to laugh or cry. "No, Quinn, I didn't take notes. I did use a highlighter, though. Hopefully that won't be the end of my law school career."

Quinn looked smug. "Oh, I'm sure you'll be fine. It's just that in Law Stars they said—"

Kraft interrupted. "OK, so, Quinn, I'm off. Libby, you need a ride?"

Libby pulled out the handle on her bag. "Nah. I'd rather walk. I don't want to put you out."

Kraft jingled his keys and gestured toward the door. "It's a small town. There's hardly anywhere we can go that's too far from anywhere else."

Libby looked at Kraft hard. "That's OK. I'm fine."

Quinn stood waiting.

"Well, good night, Quinn!" Kraft booked it toward the door.

Libby looked at Quinn apologetically. Sure, the woman had a thing about plugs and was kind of obsessive about her notes, but she didn't deserve for Kraft to brush her off like that. "Have a good night, Quinn. Don't stay up too late reading."

"Night," Quinn replied. "Hopefully not. I only have nine six-minute blocks left. Then I'm supposed to sleep. That's what they said in Law Stars."

"You do that, then. See you tomorrow." Libby waited a beat until Kraft had disappeared, then followed him out the door.

•   •   •

Connie unlocked the front door of her Craftsman-style cottage and called out. "Felix! Where are you, buddy?"

A seven-pound wiener dog sprinted to the foyer and stopped by the table where Connie kept her keys and mail.

"Were you sleeping, boy? Your fur is looking pretty ratty."

Felix Frankfurter gave Connie a wary look.

"Yeah, I'm sorry. I know I shouldn't tease you about your fur.

How's this? It's the nicest, wireiest, reddest fur in Newport."

Felix sat back on his haunches.

"OK, so I'm forgiven. Let's get some sleep, boy. I can't believe I stayed out with your Auntie Sarah until 11:00. On a school night! I haven't done that since my last date with that loser dude about a million years ago! Uncle James would be cheering!"

Connie headed to the bedroom. Felix trotted along behind, then stopped at a closed door halfway down the hall. He whimpered.

"He's not there, boy. He's not going to be. It's been five months. I'm starting to worry that you're not ever going to give up."

Felix met her eye. He sized her up. She gestured toward the back door.

"But you can go out to the backyard and mark your territory before bed if you want to. Gotta make sure that no squirrels are out there messing with your yard."

Connie could have sworn that Felix nodded. He trotted to the back door.

Connie looked back at the closed bedroom door. She took one step toward it. She stopped.

"Nope, Connie, gotta move on."

She opened the back door, called Felix in, and headed in to bed. A good night's sleep would help both of them forget for a little while.

Six

"So," Connie continued. "What we're talking about here is the intersection of law and justice." Connie clicked to the next slide. A giant photo of a marble building filled the screen. Above the front doors, an inscription read, "Equal Justice Under Law."

"Anyone know what this building is?"

Connie looked around. A few students were looking at their computer screens. One or two were typing. Most of the rest were just trying not to meet her eye. Ms. Behl, on the other hand, was staring at the PowerPoint screen, a look of confusion on her face. Connie was just about to call on Mr. Matthews — no one in the entire room was volunteering — when Ms. Behl started to raise her hand, seemed to change her mind, then put it up high.

Connie thought about whether she should make someone else volunteer today, but then she shrugged.

"Ms. Behl?"

"Um. So. I'm pretty sure that's the Supreme Court?"

Connie smiled. This one was confirming initial impressions, unlike Kraft, who seemed to be trying to do a back bend on the back bench, his chest was pushed out so far.

"Yep. It's the Supreme Court. Some of you might have heard of it?"

The class tittered. Everly typed furiously. Heard . . . of . . . it. On the right side of the room, about halfway up, Mr. Matthews nodded his head.

"That's the motto across the front of the United States Supreme Court. Now, you can't actually go in through that door, it's true, and that's a whole 'nother discussion about law and justice, but it's still there, facing the street and the Capitol building, for everyone who passes to see.

"What does that mean? 'Equal Justice Under Law'?"

Ms. Behl was quiet. Connie liked that. It meant she was pondering and wasn't just tossing her hand in the air to offer some kind of off-the-cuff answer to every question. Law was about thinking. Connie's job was to make her students discover that thinking was fun.

Everly raised her hand. "I think it means that law comes first? That justice is under it?" Her voice quivered just a bit. She'd never volunteered in class before, and Connie could tell that she wasn't sure she ever would again. Some students — like Everly, she suspected — could not handle that feeling of being exposed. No, they preferred being buried in their notes. From what Connie could see, to Ms. Everly, in her notes, everything was sure.

But Kraft was on board with Everly's answer. "Right. What Quinn said. It's kind of like we were talking about last time. You gotta have rules. If it turns out that the rules seem unfair for someone, well, they just have to deal."

"But, I don't know . . ." Ms. Behl chimed in, with a smirk toward Kraft. "Because the very first words are 'Equal Justice.' Isn't that trying to say that justice is available to everyone? I mean, it should be. And I thought that was what the Supreme Court was trying to ensure."

"Huh," said Connie. "So, Ms. Behl, you don't think that the 'under law' thing means anything?"

Everly's typing echoed in the quiet room as Behl considered.

Means . . . anything.

"I think it does. I think it means that the Justices will use the law to make sure that justice is done."

"Ah, but whose version of justice?" Connie asked. "Did your homework assignment make you think about that?"

Kraft raised his hand high. "Well, yeah. Because, like, maybe a school thinks it's just or maybe fair to kick a guy out just because some girl said he did something, but she can't prove it, and he didn't do it. But maybe the guy thinks that he should be able to stay because the bit — I mean, the girl is full of shit and pathetic, and it's his campus, too."

In the middle of the room, a woman named Patel and a man named Lee looked at each other. Ms. Jackson looked down at her desk and covered her mouth. Connie could read their faces. This kind of disrespect for people — even hypothetical people, and maybe not even hypothetical, if Connie's gut was right — was kind of horrifying.

"OK," Connie admonished. "Let's try to refrain from name calling."

Kraft took a deep breath. He nodded. "I meant, it's a pathetic situation."

Connie continued. "So, did your group have a conversation similar to this one?"

Ms. Everly jumped to raise her hand. Connie could tell she knew the answer to this one. "Um, yeah, you wouldn't even have believed how long we sat there talking about this. Libby was all like, but that poor woman! How can we possibly think she's lying? Why would she do that? And Anderson was so totally trying not to tell Libby she was wrong. But he kept talking about what if the guy was just being nice and what if he misinterpreted and what if the girl was drunk and he said/she said . . ."

"We were totally there for *hours*. Like, I had to use 40 of my six-minute blocks for the day."

Connie nodded. "You think four hours is a lot? Welcome to the rest of your life. Good legal thinking takes time. And it sounds like this was a pretty intense conversation."

Ms. Everly nodded. "Wow. You did that math really fast."

Connie did a double-take. Did Everly really think that a law professor couldn't multiply? Now, dividing was a problem, that was true. Sarah always had to calculate the tip when they went out. Actually, that had been James's specialty.

Stop thinking about James, Connie scolded herself. Get the class wrapped up.

"Yes, Ms. Everly, I did graduate from third grade, thanks."

"And, well, there went another fascinating seventy-five minutes. Be sure to meet with your groups for the next assignment. Sounds like the Behl/Kraft/Everly group is on a roll."

"Wait," asked Ms. Behl. She looked up at Connie. "You mean . . . our groups . . . for the first assignment . . . are our groups for the whole semester?"

"Nope," Connie answered. Behl sagged in relief.

"The whole year, actually. Have fun. Ciao for now."

•   •   •

Libby had been pretty darn sure that that photo had been of the Supreme Court, even if she'd never noticed the motto before. It was only her favorite place on earth. Everything was routine and expected there. It happened in a systematic way. It was based on tradition. People acted like you thought they would. That was the way it had to be, Libby thought. Or else her whole vision of the Supreme Court — Justice O'Connor smile and all — was going to go down the tubes here at law school.

What Libby couldn't believe was that she'd been the only one in the entire class to recognize the façade of the building that was, to her, an icon. Why were all of these other 1L's here?

Libby put the thought out of her mind and headed for Legal Grounds. If she didn't get some caffeine twenty minutes ago, she was going to spontaneously combust.

She felt a hand on her shoulder, pulling her back. Her books and laptop went in twenty different directions. The lid on her to-go mug went flying. As she turned to catch it, the last three tablespoons of coffee ended up all over . . . Anderson's pink button-down.

"Wow, Anderson, thanks," Libby frowned. "That was just what I needed, after that class. Could you lay off on the touching me all the time? I'm not much of a touchy feely person, OK?"

"Look, I'm sorry," Anderson said, stepping back several giant steps and wiping his shirt with his hands. "I just wanted to see if you wanted to grab a bite or something. And maybe talk about ILT. I'm so hosed in that class.

"But I'm getting the sense that I just hosed myself even more. And with something even more important than ILT. With the great Liberty Behl."

Libby took two steps even further back. "You know, Anderson, I really need a break. And some coffee. And some relative peace. In that order. As soon as I can grab all of my stuff from where you sent it crashing into the far reaches of the law school. So, bye for now."

"OK, look, I get it. Can I make it up to you? Take you out on Friday night? The JPT has one of those stage-to-screen shows going. I'm pretty sure it's Shakespeare this time."

"I'm not really the Jane Pickens Theater type. I'm more of a 'sit at home and read about the Supreme Court' kind of girl. But thanks anyway."

"Well, hey, I can read about the Supreme Court with the best of them. Got a book you can lend me?"

"Sorry, no. I've got them all lined up on my bookshelf, and the others would feel lonely if one of them went out to play with you. I'm heading out now. See you at study group, Anderson."

Libby picked up her laptop from the floor, then smiled in thanks at Matthews, the loafers guy, who had appeared from inside the classroom to collect her casebook and notebooks, and headed down the hall. She tried not to stomp.

The front door of the Supreme Court would be reopened as an entrance before she'd go out with Anderson Kraft.

•   •   •

At Legal Grounds, Libby sat at a tiny table in the back, a giant coffee in front of her. She relaxed for what felt like the first time all day, probably because no one from ILT was anywhere to be seen. Not Quinn (so there were plenty of plugs available), not Anderson (hopefully he'd given up?), not even Matthews (who seemed like one of the only normal people in this law school, even though he just came and went on little cat feet). Libby needed to vent. She emailed her father.

From: Libby Behl <lbehl@warrenlawschool.edu>
To: Angel Behl <abehl@foodandtravelwriters.com>
Date: September 5, 2014, 11:34:02
Re: Where in the world is Angel Behl?

Hey, Dad.

Where are you these days? Last I heard, you were swimming with whale sharks in Cancun. I'm guessing that you didn't perish or I would have gotten a call from the State Department or something. Unless the PR folks somehow managed to cover up the incident? I'm picturing the scene — prominent travel writer swallowed by whale shark while on press trip with four other journalists. A publicist's worst nightmare. Stock photo of eaten journalist pasted into group photo at end to evade disaster detection.

Anyhow. Assuming you are alive and well and somewhere on one of the seven continents . . . Did you say something about Rome? Or Athens? I forget.

I'm so not sure about this law school thing. I mean, I sort of like the thinking part. Actually, I have this class called Intro to Legal Thinking. I'm pretty sure what we're doing is debating legal philosophy. It's all like — when should law win? When should justice win?

And, actually, the prof in that class is almost cool. I think you'd dig her. She's pretty much totally your type. Petite, blond, brilliant. Like my mom was. Not sure if the prof is into scuba diving or heli-skiing. Otherwise, you'd be star struck.

But the other students are just plain off the charts weird. My study group is like a bad comedy routine. There's this one guy who's all "I went to Harvard so I am cocky as hell," who thinks that women ask for men to be rough with them, then there's this woman who's all about writing every single word down, but she doesn't seem to be processing any of it.

But then, I'm not writing that much down. Pretty much all I'm doing is processing. Am I doing it right? Does writing help you process? Or does it get in the way?

You're the writer. You tell me.

Miss you.

Libby

Libby took a big gulp of coffee. Now, to try to get through the assignment for Contracts. Maybe this assignment would be more doable than the ILT paper she was putting off. She was pretty sure she knew what restitution was — hadn't her dad gotten it once when the cruise ship he'd been on had broken down and the toilets hadn't worked for something like three days? She had blocked out whatever he'd told her about pooping in his workout socks. Yes, yes she had. OMG, suddenly reading about restitution was sounding so much better than letting her brain run wild.

•   •   •

Libby looked at the clock. How had it gotten to be midnight already? She'd been reading Contracts all day, but she hadn't even gotten to Civ Pro. And Quinn had circulated a transcript of their group meeting from a couple of days ago, but Libby hadn't had a chance to read through it all and see if there was anything they could turn into a group reflection paper.

"Breyer, can you stop swimming in circles for a minute and help me out here?" Libby looked through the glass of the fish bowl sitting on her desk. "You're six years old. That's got to be, like, sixty in gold-fish years. You have any wisdom for me about how to get Anderson to keep his hands to himself and make Quinn actually talk instead of type?"

An orange speckled goldfish with fancy fins swam into his tiny courthouse lair. Libby waited. Breyer did not swim back out with an answer.

"I never should have bought you that lair, you ungrateful beast. What, you want to live on Fifth Avenue? With a new fishy home every week? I'm a law student. A poor one. Ten bucks, one courthouse lair, that's what you've got.

"Still, Breyer, it would be super nice if I could wake up tomorrow morning and find that you'd written that ILT paper for me while I slept. What do you think, bud? Can I tempt you with some bloodworms?"

Across the room, Libby heard someone shout out, "Oyez, oyez," Supreme Court speak for "Hear ye, hear ye." She had email.

Two emails, actually.

She opened the one from her father first.

From: Angel Behl <abehl@foodandtravelwriters.com>
To: Libby Behl <lbehl@warrenlawschool.edu>
Date: September 6, 2014 21:52:03
Re:Re: Where in the world is Angel Behl?

Salve, *Pulchra Filia Mea*,

Well, that's all the Latin I know. And I had to pay a Roman war-rior in chain mail two euro to get him to type that into my phone for me. Do you think he was a real warrior? That would make for a great interview for my story.

How he knows Latin is unclear, because after three days in this fair city, I am starting to get the sense that they no longer speak Latin here in Rome, but I'm assuming he did not just call you a homely hag.

Here is what I hope he said: Hello there, my beautiful daughter, from only slightly less beautiful Rome.

Probably I should have had him type "brilliant" daughter instead. What is all this "I'm so not sure about this law school thing"? How the heck do you think you are supposed to be sure at this stage? You've been there for less than a week. Believe me, back in the early days of my travel writing career, when I was covering Tallahassee and Cleveland, I was "not so sure" about this "travel writing thing." You've got to build up your expertise and your experience, pookie.

OK. You hate it when I call you that. I'll revert to "*puglia filia*."

As for writing helping you process things? For me, it's like I have ten little brains in the tips of my fingers. I never know what I'm thinking until I write it. But it's different for everyone. You'll see, grasshopper, how it works out for you. But I seriously doubt that doing your best imitation of a court stenographer is going to help you process the material.

You know, the whole justice thing pretty much started here in Rome. Or at least they sort of formalized it. Their constitution was a model for a bunch of modern constitutions.

Tell *that* to your Intro to Legal Thinking professor. You'll impress her. (I know because she does sound like my type. And a little bit like your mom. Wouldn't *that* be nice?)

I'm going to throw a coin in the Trevi Fountain for you and make a wish that the grody Harvard boy leaves you alone. Maybe I'll throw in another coin for Ms. Types-A-Lot? It sounds like she might need it.

Meanwhile, my lovely, carry on. And remember . . . Rome wasn't built in a day.

Ciao for now.

Dad

Libby grinned. Her dad was never dull, that was for sure. She just wished he'd included a selfie with the Roman warrior in chain mail.

She also wished he'd remembered that the Romans *were* known for their system of justice, but they were also pretty fond of throwing

Christians to the lions. And legend had it that they found the resulting massacre quite entertaining.

Libby opened the second email. It was from some random guy she'd never heard of, but he had a Warren Law School email address.

Oh, yeah. From the sounds of it, he was someone important. Assuming a "Dean of Students" was important.

From: Bob Cerny, Dean of Students
        <bcerny@warrenlawschool.edu>
To: All Students
        <law-students-l@lists.warrenlawschool.edu>
Date: September 6, 2014 22:32:09
Re: Power Hungry

Dear Students,

I know that we are teaching you to be "powerful" lawyers, but in doing so we did not intend for you to take us so literally that you become actual "power hogs." My imaginary dictionary, which I consult as needed in dealings with students, defines "power hog" as a student who believes it is his or her right to simultaneously occupy multiple power ports in the law building or library to the detriment of his or her classmates.

While power hogs may believe that their electrical needs outweigh the electrical needs of others, I think the law school community is best served by power sharing, or to paraphrase John Lennon (for you younger students — he was a Beatle) "Power to the people, power to [all] the people, right on."

Only use the outlets you truly need, right on,

Bob Cerny, Dean of Students

Libby hooted. Apparently Quinn had been hoarding plugs all over town. Linus had his security blanket, Quinn had her power brick. She opened a new email to tell her father (hopefully before he got eaten by lions in Rome) that the Warren Law School Dean of Students not only sounded hilarious, but was a Beatles fan.

But then "Oyez, oyez" sounded again.

Libby groaned. The "From" line read "Anderson W. Kraft."

Libby held her finger over the delete button.

But what if it was about the group reflection paper?

Did she really want to deal with this tonight?

Libby thought that being in Rome and thrown to the lions sounded better than this.

"I'll just read whatever he has to say, and then we're going to bed — right, Breyer?"

Breyer was still in his tiny courthouse. Libby wondered whether he was snoring in there.

"Thanks, dude. You're a lot of help. Guess I'm on my own."

Libby double-clicked.

> From: Anderson W. Kraft
>   <akraft@warrenlawschool.edu>
> To: Libby Behl <lbehl@warrenlawschool.edu>
> Date: September 7, 2014 00:19:12
> Re: Wisdom
>
> Hey, Libby,
>
> Been feeling so badly all day about our conversation in the hallway at school. I shouldn't have grabbed your shoulder. And I should have heard you when you said you weren't up for going out. I just want to tell you that "Wisdom too often never comes, so one ought not to reject it merely because it comes late."
>
> Forgive me?
>
> Anderson

Libby sat, staring at the email. Really? He had done that? For her? *Anderson?*

He'd actually found a book about the Supreme Court and sat down to read it? Because that part about "wisdom too often never comes" was a totally classic line from a dissent by Justice Frankfurter. In an estate tax case, no less. It was iconic. And perfectly rendered. Anderson W. Kraft could practically go to an American Constitution

Society event and fit right in. Especially if he threw on a crumpled tie and put his hand up to his forehead in frustration a lot.

Anderson. Had. Read. *Henslee v. Union Planters National Bank.* To apologize.

It even sounded like a real apology. Sort of like the one Congress had issued back in 1982, apologizing for the Japanese internment camps and the Supreme Court decision upholding them.

Libby read it again, then closed her laptop, checked the lock on her apartment door, and pulled on an old T-shirt. She was going to have to sleep on that one. Maybe, when she woke up in the morning, the key to law school — not to mention the key to comprehending Anderson Kraft — would be in Breyer's bowl.

Seven

This week, of all weeks, Libby needed to distract herself. It was either that, or cry. Crying wouldn't get her reading for class done. In fact, it would give her such a headache that she wouldn't be able to think until morning. She could read all the conspiracy theory websites, but that would just piss her off.

That was why she was reading *Slate*. It made her laugh. That Dahlia Lithwick was something else. She said everything Libby was thinking, but in a funny, smart, clever way that Libby could never hope to emulate. A case in point — Dahlia (Libby liked to think they were besties, on a first-name basis) perfectly encapsulated, in one tiny paragraph, just what needed to be said about the Supreme Court: "One possible explanation for the blossoming dysfunctionality of the current Supreme Court is that the Order Muppets have all but taken over. With exception of Justices Breyer and Antonin Scalia, the Order Muppets are running the show completely . . . Remember the old rule of thumb: Too many Order Muppets means no cookies for anyone."

Too many Anderson Krafts meant no justice for anyone. After several days in which Kraft had followed Libby around, pretending to be a wild and crazy Chaos Muppet instead of owning his way-too-anal Order Muppethood, Libby had reminded herself that she just needed to stay far, far away. She was here to make sure that history could never repeat itself, not to make friends. Or boyfriends. God.

That was what she had decided today, anyway. Yesterday, in study group, she'd felt like a Quinn wannabe. She'd even almost put on a dress to go to C & B. Then she'd wondered whether her latest tumble — down the law school library stairs, arms full of treatises — had given her some kind of weird, judgment-altering concussion. Anderson Kraft was not cute.

He wasn't.

He *wasn't*.

Except when he wore that blue button-down.

Arrgh.

Staying away was always the best plan. Because, God knew, Libby did *not* want to give Anderson the wrong idea.

Libby clicked over to a website that claimed the 9/11 attacks were really a U.S. government plot. And then she did what she always did. She started commenting up a storm, telling the idiots online how full of shit they were.

•   •   •

Anderson sat on Nana's deck, reading the next assignment for ILT and trying to keep the dizziness that was panic from bubbling up. He fixed his gaze on a sailboat, bobbing in the wind, swaying side to side. On a boat, he was comfortable — he knew exactly how to grab the tiller and push it away from him, pull in the main line and let the mainsail catch the wind to the verge of a luff. There was nothing like that feeling of freedom — freedom he controlled.

And he had been pretty sure he knew how to do this law school thing, too, except that, a little over a week in, waves kept swelling up where he didn't expect them to, threatening to capsize his boat. How did Libby know so much about the Supreme Court, when he didn't have a clue? Was he supposed to know that stuff already? Was there some secret book all the other students had been reading over the summer? He'd thought he'd come to law school to learn about the Supreme Court and how justice worked and how laws were passed — all the better to make sure he knew how to defend himself if he needed to — but it seemed like he was adrift at sea and way behind, to boot. Libby was getting it, that was clear. Even if Quinn wasn't totally getting it, at least she took great notes. Anderson? He got nothing.

At least Libby probably didn't realize that you could Google "Justices admit making mistakes" and come up with insanely on-point and persuasive quotes by Justice Frankfurter.

Anderson shifted in his seat and tried to focus on the book in his lap. All he needed was for Nana to come out and find him tapping his foot furiously on the ground, taking deep breaths, trying to concentrate. She'd probably start saying what she'd been saying for years: that Anderson's personality wasn't really suited for law school, that he needed to find a career where he could feel relaxed and confident, not pressured and stressed. She might even tell him that there was still time to get a refund for the semester — and it was her money, after all. She might tell him that feeling challenged brought out his worst qualities.

He was not going to have that conversation again. He'd had to have it about a million times since the thing in college. And, even if Nana was usually right, on this point, she was wrong. He could do this. And even if things got worse and he was truly lost, instead of a bit confused, he was going to put that confident Anderson image out there. He knew how to sell it. He'd been doing it for years. And often, most of the time in fact, he could get others to buy it.

OK, "others" didn't usually include Nana. But if she did catch on that he was worried and he refused to talk about dropping out of law school, she'd probably suggest a sail. And that might help, if nothing else did. When the wind whipped through his hair and he got his hands on the wheel, he'd find his center.

And then he'd use that center to figure out how to get Libby to help him — and make her think it was a privilege, to boot.

The panic was lifting.

·   ·   ·

Connie and Felix were walking along the water. The wind was blowing hard enough to make Felix's ears blow across his eyes. He shook his head, then barked at some ducks, then looked up at Connie with an irritated look when they quacked at him and pooped in his path. Connie's empirical studies of Felix's taste preferences had confirmed her anecdotal observations that duck poop was not nearly as tasty as cat poop. Now, if a cat were to wander by . . . then Felix would be in heaven, but Connie's arm would be yanked off by the excitement of it all.

Arms weren't all that were being yanked today. A loud voice yanked Connie out of her meditative peace. It was the angry, annoyed voice of a cocky young man.

"Hey, mutt, could you shut the hell up? Some of us are trying to study up here!"

Connie turned away from the water, squinted into the sun, and looked up at a weathered wooden deck a story above her. A young man with a Harvard sweatshirt and what looked like a law school casebook was sitting there.

Could it be . . . was that really . . . how dare he.

Before Connie could speak, Anderson Kraft called out. "Oh, my gosh, Professor Shun, I am so, so sorry. I didn't realize that was you. It's just that I'm trying to get through this reading you assigned, and . . ."

Connie was weary. When would students learn that their actions would inevitably catch up with them, especially in a small town like Newport and a tiny state like Rhode Island? For hell's sake, when

James had told his barber last year how fed up Connie was with her dog groomer's inability to give Felix a decent nail trim, it had turned out that they were first cousins, even though they lived on opposite ends of the state. The next time she'd headed to Puppy Pedicures, she'd gotten the hairy eyeball from her dachshund's nail technician. And that manicurist had put a pink bandana on Felix at the end, when he was decidedly and obviously a boy.

Just like Connie was always telling Felix, it was important to be pleasant to everyone. And when "everyone" turned out to be your law professor, you hopefully figured that out pretty quickly. You just couldn't flip off your professor when she was slow to start moving at the green light because she was adjusting the volume on the radio. You just couldn't scream at your professor's dachshund on the beach. You just had to be a decent human being. Connie might not have marshals and sheriffs like Sarah did, so she couldn't use handcuffs and firearms to enforce the principle, but then, her students weren't supposed to be accused felons, either.

That was one reason — only one, it was true — why Connie was so reluctant to be forthcoming and open about her life when she was talking to students.

"No problem, Mr. Kraft," Connie answered, gritting her teeth and smiling. "Just remember that this is a public beach. There are a lot of dog walkers down here. Maybe you'd find it quieter in the library." Connie kept walking. Felix turned around, looked up at the deck, and growled, then barked. Her face turned toward the water, Connie smiled. You tell him, Felix, she thought. And then she let her thoughts turn back toward quiet, and wind, and the very finest of Swiss chocolate.

•   •   •

Libby and Anderson were sitting in C & B, waiting for Quinn to show up. Libby looked at her watch. It was only 5:57. She figured they couldn't expect Quinn for at least another three minutes. Knowing Quinn, she had scheduled two six-minute blocks to walk from her apartment to the bar, and she hadn't wanted to close her laptop a single second early.

Anderson was tapping his foot in a way that a month ago had been annoying but now was sort of endearing. Libby wasn't sure what to make of that. Usually, with a guy, she either liked his rhythm, or she didn't. She either admired his facial hair, or she didn't. She either raised her fist in solidarity with his politics, or she didn't. He either wore Birkenstocks (good) or Nikes (not as good) or wingtips (not nearly as good).

Anderson was clean-shaven and wore orange Converse hightops. And those were just two of many ways in which Anderson was outside of Libby's comfort zone.

Libby just needed to remember a basic truth of feminism: She didn't need a guy. Even though her mom had married her dad, she had done the hero thing all on her own. Justices Kagan and Sotomayor weren't married, and they beat up on the guys all the time, in their opinions, anyway.

Guys could be real trouble.

Maybe the reason Libby was resisting Anderson's shoes — and his smile, and his clean-cut good looks — was because he made her unsure of all that.

It seemed like law school was making her more uncertain about what she thought and believed rather than less. Libby had come to law school determined to do justice, just like Justice O'Connor. To make the world a better place for women, who shouldn't have to wear burkas or be date raped or be sexually harassed at work or make seventy-seven cents on the dollar. She'd seen way too much of that crap in her travels around the world, even in beer halls right here in fair New England.

Whom was she kidding? Libby had come to law school to try to be more like her mom. To help people who needed her, even at the ultimate cost.

And she still thought that law school was probably the best place to learn how to make the world a better place.

The great thing about law school? Libby liked being stimulated all the time. The sucky thing? She didn't like how it made her question everything she believed in, including the fact that dating a cute guy in your section was nothing but a distraction. That dating any guy was asking for trouble. Once upon a time, her only wavering had been about whether she wanted to be a women's rights lawyer (like Ruth Bader Ginsburg) or an advocate for abortion rights (like Kate Michelman) or an incisive legal journalist who covered important issues like individual rights (like Linda Greenhouse). Or a prosecutor who took out the terrorists, one by one. Yeah, that.

In terms of holding her interest, law school was the bomb. Some mornings she woke up and remembered that she'd been dreaming about jurisdiction or negligence or battery. It might sound geeky (it certainly would to Anderson, she suspected), but she liked the jurisdiction dreams. For one thing, she didn't wake up in a cold sweat after dreaming about whether a court could hear a case or not. For another thing, when she dreamed about that day, and her mom, and the unending news coverage, and the grounded flights, and the inability to get home and *find her mom*, she needed comforting. And then she started thinking about who should be comforting her. And it wasn't Breyer.

Being stimulated by school was good. But now being stimulated was taking on a whole new meaning. As in, the guy next to her was constantly on her mind, starting with that moment in the morning when she woke up all hot and bothered. Did Ruth Bader Ginsburg think about love a lot, back before her husband died? Or did he just cook her dinner and rub her feet so that she could go about her business of fighting for feminism? Way back when, did her mom daydream about kissing her dad's soft lips? Ew. OK. Libby wasn't going there.

But the real question was this: Was it anti-feminist to wonder what Anderson looked like without a shirt on? Was it just plain dumb? These were not the kinds of questions that Libby wanted occupying her mind. And they certainly weren't the questions she'd come to law school to ask.

Anderson kept tapping his foot, but now it was to the beat of the music on the jukebox. Someone had apparently decided that it was a Rod Stewart "If You Think I'm Sexy" kind of night.

Libby glanced over at her study partner, who was now so absorbed in the music that he was rolling his shoulders and snapping his fingers. He felt her gaze and smiled, then turned to her and held out a hand. "Dance?" Libby felt a grin creeping on to her face. They couldn't dance in here. No one danced in C & B. On the other hand, no one but their group studied in here, either. This music was so . . .it made Libby feel so . . . oh, why the hell not. They were in public. There were tons of people around. It wasn't like she was going to take her nice, loose clothes off or anything. Libby stood and reached across the table to Anderson.

And then she felt a tap on her shoulder.

Quinn was standing there, looking from Anderson to Libby, hugging her laptop to her chest. "So, what did I miss?"

Right. It had been three minutes. Libby collapsed in her chair and tried to take a deep breath without letting Quinn or Anderson see.

The song on the jukebox changed. Katy Perry. Better.

Wait. Maybe not. Libby did not want to think about going all the way tonight. Not at all.

Libby had been wrong. Nightmares didn't happen at night, and they weren't about negligence and murder. A real nightmare was sitting here, in this bar, with these people, with this song playing. A real nightmare was this: starting to sweat when Quinn gave her the hairy eyeball, starting to shiver when Anderson looked at her meaningfully, and starting to swear at the thought of all the work they had to accomplish tonight. Shun had given them an assignment. It was massive. It had to do with *To Kill a Mockingbird.*

Libby only wanted to kill this mood.

On impulse, she stood up. "I'm so sick of this place," she said. "I need a change of scene. How about we try Legal Grounds tonight?"

Quinn looked over at Anderson and frowned. "It will take us at least six minutes to walk over there."

Anderson looped his arm through Quinn's and gave her a toothy smile. "It's OK. Libby will tell us all about the book on the way."

Libby breathed a sigh of relief. In the fresh, cool, fall air, she could settle down. She didn't even mind that, apparently, she was going to have to explain the most quintessential book on justice ever written to these two clueless study group partners of hers. At least maybe this way, Anderson's attention would shift to Quinn.

And then Libby thought again. Wait. Maybe Anderson's attention would shift to Quinn. Her heart sank.

Out of here. Now.

Libby grabbed her backpack and pointed toward the door. She gestured to Anderson and Quinn. "Legal Grounds?"

Quinn pulled Anderson along. "Let's go fast!"

As they left the bar, someone turned up the jukebox.

Eight

Ten days into ILT, and Connie was pretty sure she had all the players down. Middle of the room: Ms. Jackson, thoughtful and a little bit militant; Ms. Patel, pretty on top of things, but not willing to display her competence to the rest of the class; Mr. Katz, struggling — possibly unprepared in undergrad? Connie made a note to look up his college transcript.

Back row: Mr. Sanders, goof off — probably going to wake up to the rigor of law school just a little bit too late, after he got his first semester grades; Mr. Kraft, overconfident, defensive, ready to attack, trying to schmooze Connie, but not smart enough to know that his approach was totally unlikely to succeed.

Front row: Ms. Everly, completely out of her depth, and pretty obviously relying on some "how to succeed in law school" book, written by a hack who wanted to make money on the backs of students who were shelling out a fortune to be here.

And then there was Ms. Behl, a possible diamond in the rough. Not to play favorites, but this woman seemed to have it all — smarts, focus, mission, sense of fairness, and motivation. The best ones — the ones Connie took under her wing — were always about more than wanting a prestigious career and beaucoup bucks. They were about solving major problems in the world. If Connie had to put money on it, she'd guess that some significant life event had driven Ms. Behl here to Warren Law.

Connie clapped her hands loudly and spoke. "OK, everyone, let's begin.

"This coming Sunday is the anniversary of 9/11. Today, I'd like to talk about some legal issues that are still percolating, thirteen years after the attacks."

Connie pressed the clicker with her thumb and looked back at the video screen behind her. A photo of a smiling, chubby man with a scraggly beard covered the wall.

"This is James Zadroga. He was a member of the NYPD, the New York City Police Department, on September 11, 2001. Detective Zadroga was the first NYPD police officer who is believed to have died as the result of breathing contaminated air at Ground Zero. He passed away four years after the attacks, in January of 2006."

Connie turned back to the class. No one was taking notes. They were all staring at the screen.

"Think about it," Connie said. "Most of you were in elementary school — what, third or fourth grade? — when the terrorist attacks happened. And now you're in law school. And people who were there on 9/11 are still dying. But there's a big controversy going on, still, this late in the game, about whether their deaths were actually caused by their exposure to bad stuff at Ground Zero or whether, as these folks have gotten older, they simply got sick like tons of other people do, through some natural process that we don't completely understand."

Connie clicked again. The wall behind her filled with a photo of the rubble at Ground Zero on the day of the attacks, an American flag flying in the wind.

"Pretty early on," Connie said, "some 9/11 first responders and volunteers started reporting that they were having trouble breathing.

They were diagnosed with various respiratory illnesses.

"One interesting fact was that a lot more women died after 9/11 than on the actual day itself, from illnesses they are thought to have contracted that day. A lot of them were first responders who weren't fire fighters or police officers, people like EMTs and paramedics.

"But the government wasn't sure what to do with them. It was fairly straightforward to set up a fund to compensate the families of those who actually died on 9/11, but how should we count those who died in the weeks and months and years afterwards?

"Thoughts?"

Ms. Jackson raised her hand, and Connie pointed at her.

"I guess . . ." Ms. Jackson said. "It's hard. Because people were really altruistic in going to Ground Zero to help out, you know? But on the other hand, it's true that they might have gotten cancer if they had just been sitting at home in their chairs, watching it on the news. My aunt got breast cancer a couple of years ago, and she was in Philadelphia on 9/11. So who's to say that it isn't just a coincidence that some people at Ground Zero got it?"

Mr. Katz spoke up, and the class turned to him. "Well, but, if they have some disease like cancer or something, isn't there some kind of test that doctors could do to see how they got it?"

Several students nodded.

"I don't think so," Ms. Jackson answered, shaking her head slowly. "When my aunt got sick, she asked the doctors whether there was anything she'd done to cause it. They told her, no, about one in eight women in the United States will develop breast cancer during her lifetime. They don't know why. They told her not to blame herself."

Ms. Patel shot her hand up in the air. Good for her, Connie thought. She's starting to come out of her shell. "And if we start saying that people are getting sick from 9/11, won't that keep people from wanting to help in these situations in the future? Maybe they'll say, 'Well, I'd like to volunteer, but I'm probably going to get cancer from it, so I think I'll play it safe.'"

Connie looked around the room. Mr. Sanders was doodling on the cover of his notebook. Mr. Kraft was rocking his seat back and forth and trying to hide his cell phone in his lap. Ms. Hall was sitting with her head rested on one hand, looking in Ms. Jackson's direction and seeming engaged. Ms. Behl was sitting very straight in the front row. She looked like she wanted to say something, but she had her lips pressed together and her hands gripped on the desk in front of her.

Connie continued. "So what you're saying, Ms. Patel, is that we should refuse to compensate people who get sick in rescue efforts because acknowledging the harm they might suffer will discourage others from aiding in other rescue situations in the future?"

Mr. Torres, a skinny guy sitting in the third row and wearing his baseball cap backwards, raised his hand. "Well, but, wouldn't the opposite be true? If people know that responders get sick but no one takes care of them or helps them financially, maybe they'd think they shouldn't risk it?"

Connie looked around the room. "What do you all think? In compensating people, should the government be thinking in terms of incentives to help in future disasters? If it thinks compensation will encourage more people to volunteer, should it come down on the side of compensation? Or should it have some other standard, some other motivation for compensating or refusing to compensate people with post-disaster health issues?"

Mr. Kraft looked up from his lap and his cell phone and spoke from the back row. "Look, if you don't require people to prove that their conditions were caused somehow by the disaster, then you're going to be giving money to a heck of a lot of people who were sick for some other reason and are cashing in on a government payday. Like, that Zadroga guy. Wikipedia says that the New York medical examiner found that he was injecting prescription drugs, and that his wife died with, like, methadone in her. If the guy was some drug addict, why should we give him any benefits at all?"

In the front row, Ms. Behl was twisting a piece of paper in her hands, white-knuckling it until it shredded, bit by bit. Connie took note. Maybe she should call on Behl to participate? Or maybe not. She looked pretty emotional. An outburst wasn't going to help anything.

Connie paused a moment to give Mr. Kraft's comment time to sink in. Then she turned back to Mr. Kraft. "So, Mr. Kraft, you're saying that people will lie to get benefits? Even police officers like Detective Zadroga?"

Ms. Jackson spoke up again. "Professor Shun, I don't know whether people in general will lie, but there are an awful lot of cases where the police lie about other stuff. Any public defender will tell you that police officers are lying sacks of shit. So I don't see how you can argue that they'll lie to get young black kids convicted of crimes they didn't commit but won't lie to get themselves money for health benefits."

Phil Nguyen, a quiet Asian-American guy Connie had never even noticed before, joined the conversation. "Well, but, how can you say that they're lying? Because if they were there on 9/11, and then they get cancer, how could they know if they got it because they breathed something in or not?"

"Huh," Connie said. "Anyone have a thought on that? Ms. Ingalls?" Connie pointed to a slight redhead sitting on the left side of the room, a woman who hadn't spoken up recently.

"But how could we know they didn't? If they can prove that they were there, and that they now have cancer, should that be enough?" Ms. Ingalls finished her point and then looked down at her desk. A red flush moved from her cheeks down her neck.

Mr. Nguyen sat up straighter in his seat. Whoa, thought Connie. This guy is a hidden cannon. "So anyone who was there and gets sick at any point should just get money? Don't we spend enough money in this country? Don't we have an awfully huge deficit? Can we really afford to keep spending without limits and without proof?"

"Ms. Ingalls?" Connie asked. The redhead looked like she was hyperventilating. Connie waited, giving her time to catch her breath but not wanting to let her off the hook. Law students needed to learn how to deal with opposition. That was kind of a bona fide job qualification, in lawyer speak.

"I'm . . . I'm not sure how we can say that spending money to help 9/11 responders is a waste. Isn't that really what you're saying, Phil?"

"I'm saying we shouldn't give them buttloads of money just because they happened to be there on 9/11 and then they happened to get sick! Are we going to do that for everyone who responded during Hurricane Katrina? Or the Station Nightclub fire that happened right here in Rhode Island, a couple of years after 9/11? What if those people get sick? Are we going to give them money, too? When? Out of what funds? Where do we draw the line?"

In the front row, Ms. Behl was kicking her foot against the leg of the desk. She probably really wanted to kick Mr. Nguyen, Connie speculated. He was arguing against compensating victims. Not totally Ms. Behl's thing.

Hands were going up all over the room. "But 9/11 was more dangerous than any other disaster we've had!" "But the heroes on 9/11 were, like, heroic!" "We don't have enough money to just hand out to people who are sick unless we know for sure why!"

Connie stood, quietly, looking at her class. On the one hand, she loved it when her students got so wrapped up in a class discussion that they didn't need her at all. They could take it away, all by themselves. On the other hand, in a class of 100 students at a New England law school, chances were that at least one of them had a close relationship with someone who died on September 11 or in the aftermath. And, whoever it was, that person might never speak in class again if Connie didn't shut this down. Part of Connie's job was knowing when to let the students go at it. Part of her job was knowing when enough was enough.

She rapped on the podium and spoke above the din. "OK, people. So some of you think the law should protect the responders who became sick afterwards. Some of you don't. The purpose of this conversation wasn't to find an answer, but to help us think about why laws are passed and why the political process in passing them can be so fraught."

Connie clicked to a photo of Barack Obama, sitting in a white polo shirt, in front of a tropical landscape. "On January 2, 2011, President Obama signed into law the 9/11 James Zadroga Health and Compensation Act. For many of the reasons you all just outlined, members of Congress fought for a long time — several years — over the bill that led to this law. And, Ms. Ingalls, the discussion we've just had should be a lesson to you and anyone else who is hesitant to speak her mind. Ms. Ingalls was spot on. The law only requires proof of a covered disease and presence at a crash site on 9/11 or in the immediate aftermath.

"In your groups, I'd like you to write 1000 words about why the final iteration of the Zadroga Act is a good compromise — or a complete waste of taxpayer dollars. And if you can't agree in your groups, remember that the folks in Congress had a pretty tough time, too."

In the front row, Ms. Behl had stopped kicking the desk. She had put down the twisted notebook paper. She was slumped in her chair, her laptop closed. She looked defeated in a way that concerned Connie. Every year, a few students who came to law school with all engines blazing just sort of petered out, lost faith. Connie hoped that Ms. Behl wasn't going to be one.

Meanwhile, as the class started to pack up its stuff, Connie heard the students chatting amongst themselves. Ms. Ingalls was standing straight and smiling. Mr. Kraft was holding his cell phone out to Mr. Sanders, apparently trying to show him something about James Zadroga on that pinnacle of all research sites, Wikipedia. Ms. Jackson was shutting down her computer and stuffing it into her backpack.

In the ruckus, Connie missed seeing Libby Behl slip out the door.

•   •   •

Libby lay on her bed, eyes closed, the Indigo Girls playing over her iHome. She wanted to believe the girl power group when they said that there was more than one answer to these questions — in law school, it was impossible even to figure out the questions, sometimes — but Libby definitely was *not* closer to fine.

She didn't know whether her grade would get marked down if she bagged out of study group and the 9/11 benefits assignment. But she did know that she just wasn't up to it. Not tonight, after the bluebird day she'd just lived through. Maybe not ever.

She texted Quinn and Anderson. **Hey terrible head8k. Can't think. Have 2 lie in dark rm. Cover 4 me on essay? Thx.**

Libby pressed "send," listened to the swoop of the journey through cyberspace, confirmed that it hadn't bounced back.

Then Libby put her phone in airplane mode, turned up the volume on her music, and shut out the lights.

Law school would still be there tomorrow. And so would the memories of 9/11.

Nine

Connie was standing beside the credenza in her office, digging through the drawers for the Hershey's Kisses she *knew* she'd left there yesterday. She was positive that she had not eaten them all. More than positive. Super duper positive.

Well, the custodial staff had emptied her trash. Even if she had eaten them all, there was no silver wrapper evidence to be found.

She sat down, pulled up Facebook, and smiled at all the likes she'd gotten for today's status update.

> Here's a link to my appearance yesterday on HuffPost Live, where I discussed recent Supreme Court developments and where Felix, that Earl Warren fan of a dachshund, made a cameo appearance to express his anti-originalist views. Yes, in fact, for a full minute of the broadcast, Felix's voice was the only one that could be heard.

Yesterday had been a hoot, to put it nicely. Today wasn't going much better. Felix had been especially grumpy this morning — was it Connie's fault that people were leaving comments on Huffington Post, telling Felix he had no idea what he was talking about? — her car had been making the kind of sound that the Magliozzi brothers loved to imitate, and her students were being way too high maintenance.

From: Connie T. Shun <cshun@warrenlawschool.edu>
To: Sarah Abernathy
        <judge_abernathy@rid.uscourts.gov>
Date: October 31, 2014
Re: Halloween tricks? Why no treats?

Hey, Your Honor,

Can you shoot me now? Oh, whoops, I don't think I'm supposed to be writing that to a judge. Will they let me in the courthouse next time I'm over there to take you out to lunch? Or will I be surrounded by armed marshals at the door? Please advise.

It has been one of those days. I got called in to see the Dean because I pissed off the copy guy by not removing staples from my documents before sending them to the copy center. Seriously? You can't make this stuff up.

Oh, and there have been several student exchanges that will amuse you, although not me: "Professor Shun, could I be first for your office hours today? I have other things I want to do." And, "I was too busy getting ready for Halloween last night to spend much time on this assignment."

Here's the icing on the cake: an email exchange I had with a student last night (cut and pasted into this single missive so as not to torture you more than absolutely necessary). So, your opinion. Do you think it is supposed to be some kind of Halloween trick?

> Professor Shun, I am at the law school to pick up my practice midterm. It is now about 8:30 p.m. and there is no one here in the admin area. I can't find my practice midterm. I really need it so I can go over it tonight. Everyone else already has theirs back, but I couldn't come earlier today, and now I think I'm at a disadvantage. I was hoping that you had commented on my work extensively so that I could review it before class tomorrow morning. What should I do? Thanks.
> *Anderson Kraft*

My assistant left them on the little table near the cubes. You can pick yours up there. *Professor Shun*

It's getting late. Could you come over and help me find it? Really, I'm trying, but I just looked around and could not find any table or any cube thingies. *Anderson*

Are you in the faculty wing? The table is right next to the cubes, which are right next to the red chairs. *Prof. Shun*

What chairs? What table? What cubes? *AK*

I came this close to saying, "The cubes are where the administrative staff members sit *during the daytime when we are all at work.* If you insist on emailing back and forth with me between 8:30 and 9:00 p.m., it is your own problem if you cannot find your practice midterm. And, no, thank you, I will not go out on Mischief Night just to help you find your paper *which you should have picked up hours ago.*"

Not that I'm feeling furious about this or anything.

James would have just rolled his eyes, reached over my shoulder, and emailed the cube-impaired student that he'd better watch out or he might be dumpster diving for his practice midterm. Then that best friend of mine would have gotten out his Buzz Lightyear costume, wrapped a Slinky around Felix's waist, shouted "To infinity . . . and beyond!", and attempted to make me try on a Jessie the Cowgirl outfit so we'd be ready to go out tonight.

If law students are this dense and self-absorbed, I shudder to think about the future of the legal profession.

At least tonight I'm likely to be able to get my hands on some chocolate. Felix has already dragged his Slinky Dog costume out of the closet for trick or treating. Luckily I'm short enough so that, if we go to a different neighborhood where no one knows us, someone might mistake me for a kid with a lasso. Wanna come along and be my mom/Mrs. Potato Head?

Connie

Connie figured that Sarah was having a crazy day. For reasons it was easy to imagine, Halloween season, and especially the day after Mischief Night, were a busy time for judges, what with a serious number of criminal defendants making their initial, sometimes sheepish appearances. In state court, they might be charged with vandalism or petty theft. As a federal judge, Sarah had to deal with truly horrific crimes like serial rape and threats to bomb a federal building. Fun times.

Connie scratched around at the back of a drawer. Eureka! She could only find two silver foil-wrapped droplets of heaven, but, hey, if a third of an ounce of milk chocolate was all that was available to an addict, she'd make it work.

Besides, it was only a few hours until she'd have an overflowing feed sack — or whatever it was that Jessie carried — of chocolately goodness. Miniature Hershey bars. Peanut butter cups. Snickers. Oh, God. It was enough to make a girl swoon. Whoever said that Halloween wasn't the best holiday was clearly in need of a chocolate reminder.

Connie sat down in her office chair, leaned back like Clarence Thomas during oral argument, and sucked on a single kiss. Slowly. Slowly. Let it melt. Actually, let the whole day melt away.

Just a few minutes before, Connie had been so worked up she could spit. Now, she could feel herself drifting off. Maybe just a little snooze would be a fine idea.

•   •   •

Anderson used his hands to apply the hair pomade. Gross. This stuff was sticky. He'd had no idea what type of hair crap Gregory Peck had used in the movie, but he figured that Axe was good for every look a twenty-first century guy could want.

Anderson straightened his dark tie, fixed the round Harry Potter tortoiseshell glasses over his face, and buttoned the vest on the tan suit he'd found in Nana's attic. It was big — he assumed it had be-longed to his grandfather in his later, portly years — but the linen was still in great shape, and the trousers were just the right length, as if he'd stepped right into Papa's pants. He stepped back from the mirror that was mounted on his dresser to take a look. Crap. He couldn't get the whole effect. He took a couple more steps back, then hefted him-self up on the bed, wobbling as he stood. He found his balance and posed with his hands in his pockets. Yep. This should do it.

If he knew Libby, she'd be more than willing to dance with war-rior-for-justice Atticus Finch, even if plain old Anderson Kraft wasn't her cup of tea.

Anderson was hoping that the Monstrous Motions and Procedural Potions Halloween dance would bring Libby and him closer togeth-er. They never got time alone — and he wasn't really thinking Quinn would give them any space tonight, either — but he was pretty sure that even Quinn wouldn't be able to dance in a threesome. He just had to wait for the right song, then be super casual when he asked Libby to dance. His ace in the hole: He'd let her get a whiff of his hair — she'd been giggling lately over some chick called Dahlia Lithwick who'd written a whole blog post or something about Axe — put his arms around her, and whisper sweet nothings about protests and jus-tice in her ear.

•   •   •

Libby scrolled through Facebook, trying to psych herself up. She couldn't believe she was doing this. She was so not the Halloween party sort. Libby liked to be able to look people in the eye, size them up, give them the once over. Masks? Not her thing.

Anderson Kraft: Do you know why witches can't have babies? Cuz their husbands have Hallow Weenies.

Angel Behl: If YOU woke up at 4:30 in the morning in a hotel in Transylvania, and your neck was on fire, and you looked in the mirror, and there was a giant bite-like thing on your neck (I am withholding the nasty details), and the thing was hot and inflamed, would you think 1) spider or 2) ant or 3) vampire?

Barton Sanders: If I wear a choir robe to be a Justice at the WLS Halloween party tonight, does that count as a costume? Or are people likely to think I'm going as a defendant in the clergy sex abuse cases?

Libby forced herself to shut down her laptop and start to think about getting dressed for this shindig.

She was pretty sure that the last time she'd been to a Halloween party had been in the Castro when she was nine. Her dad had been on assignment to cover the world's greatest Halloween parade, and he'd decided that she was old enough to appreciate the awesome crazy party that was the city's gay neighborhood on its favorite day of the year. She'd begged for stilettos and a crazy wig, but her father had explained that only boys could wear those. It had been years before she'd really understood.

What she *had* understood back then was just that, if you ate too many candy apples and followed them up with nine or ten dozen mini candy bars and a few glasses of bug juice, you were going to barf instead of parade in the streets of the Castro.

On the phone from New York, her mom had coached her dad through administering the BRAT diet: bananas, rice, applesauce, and toast. By the next morning, Libby had been feeling like herself again.

But her father's "experience is the best teacher" philosophy had sort of been right. Just one look at the Kool-Aid mascot, and her tummy felt queasy to this day.

Although she still wished she could pull off the stilettos and wig.

Especially because sometimes it would be so nice to pretend to be someone else.

Libby looked over at Breyer, whose only interest in the whole Halloween thing had ever been getting extra bloodworms. There was that Halloween night a few years back when he'd tried to throw himself from his bowl onto the table below, but Libby refused to think of that as a suicide attempt. No, Libby was pretty sure it had just been his fishy attempt to save her life after she choked on a piece of Laffy Taffy. If so, it had worked. She'd screamed so loudly at the sight of his flying, then gasping, piscine self that the death-in-waxed-paper disguised as banana goodness had erupted from her windpipe and landed in his bowl.

"Remember that, dude? I had to use the little net to scoop the nasty taffy out and put you back in. Then you swam around sucking H_2O. Either you were trying to show off your EMT skills or you really just wanted some sugar-flavored tank water. I'm giving you the benefit of the doubt."

Libby stripped down, then pulled on her Halloween get-up. She looked at herself from several angles in the mirror on the back of her bathroom door.

Breyer swam around in circles, never looking in Libby's direction.

"Oh, I get it. Deny, deny, deny," she said. "Or is it that my Lady Justice outfit isn't working for you? I'm not totally sure how I'm going to dance in this toga thing, much less with a blindfold on, but the scales totally make the look."

Breyer swam into his courthouse. "Thanks, dude. So, you don't want to look? You don't have to. Maybe I'll just forget about your Halloween color bright food flakes."

Breyer peeked out.

"Or maybe I'll come home too late for your flakes."

Breyer's fins waved out the windows.

"Or maybe I'll take you along in your bowl and let Anderson do some kind of frat boy goldfish swallowing stunt."

Breyer swam out, his eyes moving rapidly from side to side. His fins flapped around erratically. He looked like he was about to cry. And even if most fish couldn't cry, Breyer was a special fish.

"It's all right, buddy. I'm just kidding around. But it is true that, if Anderson and Quinn have anything to say about it, I'll be back late, so here are your treats now."

Breyer swam around in ever-faster circles. Then he scooted to the top of his tank and started gulping. Bloodworms were a once-a-year treat. He had to get 'em while he could. Libby hid a smile — Breyer hated it when he thought he was being mocked — and put on her blindfold. She couldn't check herself out in the mirror, but she could pretend she didn't see her goldfish pigging out on the fishy equivalent of peanut butter fudge.

•   •   •

OK. Wearing nothing but a toga (actually a bed sheet) on an evening river cruise on Halloween was kind of a terrible idea, now that Libby thought about it. Well, a camisole and boy shorts under the toga, but still. People could see her legs. And her arms. The extra-long 200-thread-count twin didn't do much to block out the wind. The metal scales were pretty cold, too. And with Libby's luck, the second she put on her blindfold for the costume parade, she'd run smack dab into a waiter with a tray full of witches' brew. Then she'd be cold, and wet, and humiliated. Plus scared. Libby hated being scared. When she was ten, she'd had enough of scared for one lifetime.

Oh, yay.

Libby rubbed her shoulders, wishing she'd decided to be a werewolf (they had fur) or a witch (they got to wear tights and hats and sometimes even gloves) or a wizard (they could wave a wand and make it warm and cozy). She tried to distract herself by looking out at the water, but the fog was so thick that she couldn't see much. If she didn't know better, she'd think that the Student Bar Association had arranged for special effects.

So, she wondered, if there was no view and the waves were toss-ing them around the way that Breyer hated when she carried his bowl across the room, what was the point of having a Halloween party on a boat? They could be inside, toasty warm, bobbing for apples and eat-ing donuts. Even better, she could be home in her secure apartment in her oldest "Give Peace a Chance" sweatshirt and pajama bottoms, trying to make a pirate costume for a goldfish and giggling about the Halloween when Chief Justice Roberts had just joined the Court and a light bulb exploded during oral argument. Giant gun-like sounds at the Supreme Court? Yeah, never a good thing. The Supreme Court police force had freaked out, but the Chief had rallied, setting every-one at ease. "It's a trick they play on new Chief Justices all the time," he joked. "We're even more in the dark than before."

Libby chortled to herself and held her scales high. "Liberty and justice for all!"

"That witches' brew getting to you, Miss Liberty Behl?"

Libby stopped and stared. This vision before her . . . it was . . . Gregory Peck reincarnated. Oh. My. God.

She felt like Ingrid Bergman.

Except that the unmatchable Ingrid would never be caught dead on a boat, in the fog, in a toga, in a blindfold, holding a set of metal scales.

But enough about that. Otherwise, they were practically identical twins.

"Anderson! Wow! When did you get here?" Libby could hard-ly speak. And it wasn't just the potion they called "witches' brew." Those tortoiseshell specs — combined with that tan linen suit — were enough to make a strong social activist weep from joy.

Anderson put his arm around Libby. "Hey there. Liberty and Lady Justice. I like it." He gave her a tiny smile and gestured up and down.

Crap. The toga was kind of gaping open. No wonder Libby had been feeling a breeze.

On the other hand, Libby was feeling much, much warmer. And, again, she didn't think it was the witches' brew.

She looked up at Anderson. She met his gaze. She thought about how amazing it would be to spend the evening kissing, and hugging, and snuggling. With Atticus Finch.

Maybe even with Anderson.

Oh, God. No.

Oh, *God*. Seriously? Quinn was wearing that?

Her black dress had rhinestones across the front, worthy of four or five six-minute blocks with a bedazzler. Her dark hair was teased, and feathered, and sprayed back from her face. She wore giant hoop earrings. And she carried a Bible and a miniature tire.

Quinn was the spitting image of Marisa Tomei in *My Cousin Vinny*. As cool, and as creepy, and as culled from the '90s, as that sounded.

She was shivering.

"Anderson, get me a drink? I'm, like, freaking out." Quinn looked pathetic. Her mascara was actually *running*.

Libby felt kind of badly for her.

"Quinn? What's wrong? I know, I'm not a huge party person, but what is there to be nervous about?"

"You wanna know what I'm nervous about? I'll tell you what I'm nervous about. I am in the dark here with all this legal crap. I have no idea what's going on."

Anderson burst out laughing.

Libby looked from one to the other. Maybe it was because the fog was getting thicker, but it was hard to see what was so funny. "Okaaaaay . . ."

Quinn said to Anderson, "Yeah, yutes like Libby don't get the reference."

Libby looked to Anderson. He shrugged his shoulders and explained. "She's just quoting Marisa Tomei. It's sort of a little game we play. We like to figure out how much of *My Cousin Vinny* we can quote from memory."

Libby was confused, and that warm feeling was quickly dispatching itself into the fog. First, why were they obsessed with a 20-year-old movie about a weird lawyer who wore a leather jacket to court? Second, when the heck were they playing this game of theirs? As far as Libby knew, the three of them were pretty much always together. Third, was Quinn kidding? She looked over-the-top depressed to Libby.

Libby decided she could ask the last question. "Look, Quinn, are you OK? Because you seem pretty upset."

Now it was Anderson's turn to be confused. He turned to Quinn. "Wait, you weren't kidding around? You really have no idea what's going on? What are you talking about?"

Quinn sniffed. Her hoop earrings swayed in the wind. She turned to the railing, stared out at the bay, and shuddered.

"The practice midterm. I bombed it. Tanked. As in, Shun wrote that she wondered whether she might help me get a tutor because I seemed confused about some fundamental concepts. And then she kept writing in the margins that I needed to go back, think about the major themes of the semester, and synthesize them. I hate synthesizers. Hate them. Techno sucks."

Libby started to break in. "I think she meant that . . ."

Quinn started to wail. "I swear. I blocked out about 40 six-minute blocks a day to study for that thing. And I'll bet you two aced it."

Libby looked to Anderson and raised her eyebrows, signaling that she'd done fine. How about him?

Anderson nodded. No problems.

Libby turned back to Quinn. "You know what? You need a potion and a dance."

Quinn wiped her eyes and straightened her dress. "You're right, Libby. Thanks so much for understanding. Let's go, Anderson." Quinn grabbed Anderson by the elbow and pulled him to the dance floor.

Now it was Anderson's turn to raise his eyebrows at Libby. He looked back over his shoulder, shrugged, then pointed to his watch. Later? Libby raised her hands, her palms upward. I don't know. Anderson waited a beat, then put his arms around Quinn and held her close.

Watching Anderson and Quinn dance cheek to cheek, Libby thought that even Lady Justice couldn't make this one turn out right.

•   •   •

Lady Justice was wilted. The scales were lying in a heap on the floor where they'd been tossed after Libby had joked to Breyer that she should weigh him and he had splashed her as hard as he could with his tail fin. *Weigh* him? After he'd eaten an entire plastic pumpkin full of bloodworms? No, thank you.

There had been no point Libby could see in staying at the Halloween ball once the boat had docked back in Newport, right after the cocktail hour. Anderson and Quinn had disappeared onto the dance floor, never to be seen again. Dancing to "The Monster Mash" just wasn't fun all alone. Line dances were supposed to be group enterprises, right?

Speaking of group enterprises, Libby wished the group could divide and conquer on the legal research assignment they'd gotten that day. Their legal writing professor was tons of fun — she laughed a lot and made learning organization and analysis interesting, as if that were even possible — but seriously? Did she have to load them up with Halloween cases to research?

Libby scrolled through Westlaw, the online legal research database they'd be using in class that week. OK, here it was. *Stambovsky v. Ackley.* A case about whether people could back out of a deal to buy a house if they later found out it was supposed to be haunted.

Libby was laughing to herself over the idea that anyone would refuse to move into a house because it was ostensibly haunted — there were dangers in this world, but Libby doubted that ghosts were among them — when her email dinged.

From: Anderson W. Kraft
        <akraft@warrenlawschool.edu>
To: Libby Behl <lbehl@warrenlawschool.edu>
Date: October 31, 2014
Re: You scared me!

Hey, Lady Justice!

Where'd you get yourself off to? Quinn and I danced a few dances and drank a few drinks, and then we turned around and you were gone.

Hey, don't take offense that we went off for a while, will you? Quinn was so down about the practice midterm. She literally cried on my shoulder. I tried to tell her that "practice" was the operative word, that even Vinny failed the bar five times before he passed on the sixth try, but she was not having any of it. She started moaning about "hating justice" and "stupid scales." It was like, keep Quinn dancing or watch her jump off a ledge.

Libs, I gotta say, whatever Quinn might have had to say about it, you were the finest Lady Justice that ever I did see. Those scales. Wow. They were seriously . . . heavy.

As in, I think Lady Justice and Atticus Finch would make a great pair, don't you? I think we should discuss. Tomorrow. Over lunch. And maybe dinner. And maybe without Quinn.

And then maybe we could talk about feelings. My feelings. Your feelings. Because, you know, Libs, "The best way to clear the air is to have it all out in the open."

Man, that Atticus Finch really knew how to say stuff. Maybe it was because the person who was giving him the words to say was a lady who was all about justice.

So, I've had a lot of witches' brew. Maybe I'm even under a spell. Your spell. Whoa. I think I like it.

Gotta go. It's the witching hour.

Anderson

So, did this mean Anderson had really wanted to dance with her, not with Quinn? That couldn't be right. Could it? Lady Justice wasn't sexy like Marisa Tomei. And the thing about Marisa Tomei, at least in *My Cousin Vinny*, was that she was deep, too. She had substance.

That seemed to be the story of Libby's life. She was smart. She was committed. She was even interesting to talk to, if you found goldfish, social justice, and the Supreme Court interesting.

But there was always some other woman who had all that plus the sizzle. Libby was the egg: full of protein, sensible, somewhat healthy. But someone like Marisa Tomei was the bacon: the yum factor, the greasy goodness, the delicious taste left on your tongue that left you smacking for more.

Most days, Libby was fine with being an egg. That was how feminists should be — they didn't need glitz and glam, just substance. And goodness knew it was safer to be plain. But tonight, of all nights, she wished she'd brought on the bacon. And that Anderson had wanted to bring her home.

Ten

Connie Shun sat in her dining room, in front of her computer, debating. Should she press "send"? Oh, what the hell. She clicked and listened to the "whoosh" as her email flew off into cyberspace.

To: ILT Students
                    <iltstudents1415@warrenlawschool.edu>
From: Connie T. Shun <cshun@warrenlawschool.edu>
Date: November 17, 2014 18:42:53
Re: Thanksgiving celebration

Students:

This year, I'm starting a new ILT tradition. Many of you may have family far away; if you can't go home for Turkey Day, please consider spending it with me.

While I'm no Rachael Ray, I've never had to call the Butterball hotline, either, so hopefully we can feast on turkey, stuffing, and all the fixings.

Three rules for Thanksgiving at my place: Must feed my dachshund, Felix Frankfurter, from the table. Must allow me to remain in denial and believe that Felix eats nothing but kibble. Must not discuss anything related to law school. As Thumper's mom once told him when he was a 1L, "If you can't keep from saying sumthin' about law school, don't say nuthin' at all."

Your professor,

Connie Shun

Connie read over her email again, then wondered whether there was a way to retract it. She really, really didn't like letting students into her personal life.

But James had always tried to convince Connie that being a professor didn't mean she couldn't be a person, too. The students might even learn something from seeing the juggling act that was a real — OK, semi-real — legal career *avec* personal life. And now Sarah was picking up the torch and bugging Connie about it.

Connie braced herself for the ping of incoming emails, all of which would undoubtedly be from eager ILT students who couldn't wait to sing Pilgrim songs around Connie's Thanksgiving table.

The silence was comforting. But Connie hit "mute" just in case.

She needed a distraction. Facebook. That would work. And she would do that upbeat Facebook thing where she made a full house for Thanksgiving sound just ducky.

Connie Shun is hoping that she gets a big, varied crowd for Thanksgiving this year and that not a single guest brings sausage stuffing. Felix gets so offended when people fail to consider a sausage dog's feelings. Plus, as you all know, John Godfrey Saxe said back in 1869, "Laws, like sausages, cease to inspire respect in proportion as we know how they are made." Felix needs all the respect he can get.

She wondered how long it would take for someone to point out that a) Felix would never know; b) any self-respecting wiener dog loved sausage, with all that fatty goodness, regardless of the pseudo-cannibalism involved; and c) most guests were more likely to show up with pie, not stuffing, anyway.

If James were here, he'd comment that he agreed with Felix. Just one more reason to be sad that James wasn't here this year. Connie's email pinged.

From: Sarah Abernathy
        <judge_abernathy@rid.uscourts.gov>
To: Connie T. Shun <cshun@warrenlawschool.edu>
Date: November 17, 2014 19:22:41
Re: I'm homeless and stuffing-less...

So, I saw that you took the plunge! Sounds like you sent out the email to your students, inviting them to "fill up the house with everything except sausage stuffing"? Don't worry, I'm coming for moral support. Can I bring a goat cheese gratin, a bottle of wine, and possibly a new man?

I'm not sure about the new man. Actually, I haven't even officially met him yet. But his profile on JudgeDate looks mighty promising, so I'm crossing all relevant digits.

Sarah the Single One

Connie laughed. There couldn't possibly be something called "JudgeDate." Could there?

From: Connie T. Shun <cshun@warrenlawschool.edu>
To: Sarah Abernathy
        <judge_abernathy@rid.uscourts.gov>
Date: November 17, 2014 19:25:36
Re:Re: I'm homeless and stuffing-less...

Um, sure on the gratin and wine. On the JudgeDate judge? You'll have to convince me. Googling just now, I found no such dating service, but given that they have them for married folks who want affairs and farmers and Trekkies, for God's sake, I'm not sure that I'll count out JudgeDate. Maybe it could sort of do a joint venture with WomenBehindBars.com?

And while we're on the subject of joint ventures, could you please help me understand why there are lonely hearts hook-ups for everyone but law professors? Are we really that esoteric and obnoxious? I know Elena Kagan never married, but I'd be fine with giving up my all-but-clinched seat on the Supreme Court if it meant that I might meet a decent man sometime in this lifetime.

Too bad James was gay. If he'd been straight, he'd be a) the father of my four adorable, due-process-loving children (you know that's what I wished for a while); b) feeding Felix under the Thanksgiving table; and c) alive.

Single and mourning,

Connie

Felix wandered into the room and started whimpering.

Connie bent down and scooped him up. "What's doing, buddy? Did you hear that Mommy has forbidden all sausage stuffing at our Thanksgiving feast? Or do you live in fear of the day that Auntie Sarah brings home a JudgeDate?"

Felix struggled against Connie's embrace and jumped down, then ran to the sliding glass door.

"Oh, I get it, you want to see if Madame Pomeranian from down the street is out and about today. OK, dude, go for it, but when she asks you whether your testicles are real or enhanced, play dumb and act like the stud you are. You do not need to offer the information that they are newsicles, purchased for you by James after what he viewed as a particularly cruel and traumatic surgical intervention."

Connie opened the door. A panting Felix went out wagging his whole body, looking from side to side. Connie got such a kick out of that dachshund's lack of coordination; most dogs could get it together to make their tails go side to side, but not Felix. No, Felix either wagged his whole hind end or circled his tail in figure eights. Connie seemed to collect the slightly flawed. Felix was no exception.

No sign of the sexy Pomeranian, but she could be waiting just around the corner. What the heck, it was a nice day out for November. Felix could lie in a sunbeam and wait. Waiting was key. If they waited long enough, maybe Connie and Sarah and Felix would all have true loves trot right up into their own backyards.

•   •   •

At study group, Libby, Anderson, and Quinn couldn't seem to focus on the last assignment Connie had given them to submit before the Thanksgiving holiday. Quinn kept spraying some kind of solvent on her screen, then testing each key on her laptop keyboard for prime bounce. Anderson seemed absorbed in figuring out just how many pigs in blankets he could stuff into his mouth at once. Libby obsessively checked her email. She wasn't sure when her dad was hitting town. Knowing Angel, it could be in the middle of the night, on top of a locomotive, with a boa constrictor wrapped around his waist to sneak it through customs.

But it was time to get this paper done and this Thanksgiving party started.

"Man, when perfected, is the best of animals, but when separated from law and justice, he is the worst of all." Libby read it out.

"What do you guys think that means? Do we even care? Or is Thanksgiving just too close?"

"I had way too much Aristotle in college, to tell you the truth," Anderson griped. "And doesn't it sound like a sort of *Lord of the Flies* type quote, anyway? Are we sure Aristotle even said it?"

"You mean you didn't Google it, Anderson?" Quinn giggled.

"Did you?" Anderson turned to Quinn and glared.

"Look, you two, we've gotta come up with something here. Do we want to go with Anderson's *Lord of the Flies* thing? Or what?"

Lord. . . of . . . the . . . Flies . . . typed Quinn.

"Well, yeah. I mean, when all those kids were just in the middle of the wilderness, they were the worst animals of all, right?" Anderson stuffed in two more pigs in blankets.

Libby was ready to give up. She tried a different tack.

"What are you guys doing for Thanksgiving?" Libby asked. "I know — I think — my dad is coming into town, but we don't have any dinner plans or anything. I'm trying to figure out whether I should take a stab at roasting a turkey."

"Why, when you can go to Shun's place for Thanksgiving dinner?" Anderson laughed. "You know you're her favorite. You'd fit right in."

"Well, I'm not sure it would be my thing, regardless. I refuse to be the only sad excuse for a student noshing on her mashed potatoes."

Quinn looked up from her keyboard. "Wait, I'll totally go if there are mashed potatoes. I love mashed potatoes. Are you sure there'll be mashed potatoes, though? Her email just said turkey and stuffing."

"And 'fixings,' Quinn. The email said 'fixings,'" Libby said patiently. "For every Thanksgiving feast I've ever heard of, 'fixings' have included mashed potatoes. Even . . ."

Quinn seemed to get it. "Oh, so is this one of those ambiguous words our professors are always talking about? Like, what's a 'motor vehicle' within the meaning of the statute? What are 'fixings' within the meaning of a Thanksgiving dinner invitation?"

"Right on, Quinn, as Dean Cerny would say," Libby agreed wearily. "You've got ILT figured out. So, are you saying we should all go?"

Quinn perked right up. She was totally getting this law school "ambiguity" thing. Aristotle, maybe not so much. But that's what study groups were for. "Well, of course! I'm in for mashed potatoes."

"Anderson?" Libby caught Harvard Boy's eye. She couldn't believe herself. She'd heard law school changed you, but she was actually considering going somewhere with Anderson? She needed a walk and talk — maybe a swim and talk? — with Breyer about this.

"Well, I guess we need a decent showing from our study group," Anderson answered. "But I'm not bringing anything. Unless she wants instant oatmeal at Thanksgiving dinner, cooking is not my thing."

Libby sighed, then made a note on her to-do list. "That's fine, Anderson," she replied. "I'll make a couple of appetizers, and you can just pretend that you contributed something. I'm not sure how that'll be that different from what you do in study group, to tell you the truth."

Quinn looked up from her spreadsheet, where she'd just recorded her total waste of two six-minute blocks while the group had debated the pros/cons of partaking in Connie's Thanksgiving feast. "Wow, Libby! That was vicious. Personally, I think Anderson contributes a lot to our study group."

"You would," Libby muttered under her breath. "He does more than transcribe every word anyone says, including 'Gotta hit the head.' "

Quinn looked over at Anderson and put her hand on his knee. "Don't worry, Andy, she's just stressed about midterms, I'll bet. I won't take what she's saying about me personally. You don't either."

Anderson pushed Quinn's hand away. "It's Anderson, Quinn. No one calls me 'Andy.' And if they did, it wouldn't be you."

"So now it starts," Libby sulked. "Every single book about law school says that study groups will start to battle with each other. And they all tell you that, when your group deteriorates to the point that it's no longer being productive, you switch study groups, do not pass go, do not collect $200. And because Shun put us in this one all to-gether, I can't avoid you two even if I try. I don't even have a chance to draw a get out of jail free card. So let's just try to get this Aristotle as-signment done and then I'm going to go home and feed my fish, who is probably starving to death and dying after six years of perfect nutri-tion while I sit here with you two and have mind-numbing conversa-tions about whether *Toy Story* nicknames still carry their weight in law school and whether mashed potatoes are fixings."

"You have a fish who has lived to be six years old?" Quinn asked, her voice amazed.

"Quinn! Just seal it!" Anderson looked furious.

"But, it's so amazing that—"

Anderson stood up and walked away from the bar table, his fists clenched. He took a deep breath and turned around.

"Libby, Quinn and I both owe you an apology."

"I didn't do any—" Anderson glared at Quinn. Quinn gulped.

"We *both* owe you an apology. You keep trying to keep us focused on the ILT assignment, and we both keep wandering off course. That's not fair to you. So, you go home and feed your fish and soak in a bubble bath, or go to a protest, or, hey! Reread that book you told me about, the one Jeffrey Toobin wrote about the Supreme Court. Quinn and I will decipher Aristotle and figure out what the hell animals have to do with law school."

"Right," said Quinn. "Or even what they have to do with me. Aristotle might have said man is the best of animals, but then we know men are animals. Women, on the other hand—"

"Thanks, Anderson," Libby interrupted. "I think I will."

Libby started out the door of C & B. Behind her, she heard chairs being rearranged, and a high, sweet voice saying, "So, Andy, this Aristotle is just so confusing! I don't understand why Professor Shun can't just assign us to watch *Orange is the New Black*. Now that would teach us something."

"Yeah, Quinn, like Piper says when her mother says she never should have been locked up because she's nothing like the other women in prison: 'I am in here because I am no different from anybody else in here. I made bad choices, I committed a crime, and being in here is no one's fault but my own.'

"Look, Quinn, we're not struggling in ILT because we're better than everyone else and we can somehow see that Professor Shun's first name is Connie because she's conning us all. We are here. It's no one's fault but our own. So let's own it.

"And I don't need your foot in my lap to own it."

Libby sputtered. Holy wow. Anderson had a spine. Who knew?

But for now, she was going to let him straighten up and show that backbone to Quinn, and only Quinn. A lock on the door, a hot bath and an hour with Toobs sounded like just the thing.

•   •   •

OK, so one hour with *The Nine* had turned into three. Or four. Libby couldn't bring herself to care. It was three days before Thanksgiving, Anderson and Quinn had handed in their final group assignment of the semester (what it said, Libby was too afraid to find out), and Libby's dad was hitting town sometime in the next 48 hours. From wherever he'd been. The Middle East, maybe?

Libby logged on to Facebook. She thought for a moment, then updated her status.

> **Libby Behl** is so psyched that Thanksgiving is Thursday and there are no law school classes until the middle of January! Let's not talk about midterms, people. That would violate the 8th Amendment.

A couple of Libby's friends posted right back.

> **Cecily Danvers:** Libby, I told you back in college that this would happen. You've turned into one of those law students who speaks legalese all the time. Translate.

> **Quinn Everly:** Yeah, translate!

> **Anderson Kraft:** She means that talking about midterms would be cruel and unusual punishment.

> **Kevin Matthews:** Talking about midterms wouldn't be punishment if it were Libby doing the talking.

Libby squinted at her screen. Kevin Matthews? Who was that? She clicked on the profile photo.

Oh, that guy Matthews from ILT. The one in the loafers. She must have accepted his friend request when the section had been organizing its end-of-the-semester potluck. Huh. He seemed nice enough, but he must be pretty blah for her not to even recognize him at this point in the semester. No, Libby thought, no one could make talking about midterms fun. Not no way, no how.

"Oyez, oyez" sounded out.

From: Angel Behl <abehl@foodandtravelwriters.com>
To: Libby Behl <lbehl@warrenlawschool.edu>
Date: November 24, 2014 22:09:45
Re: Ta ra ra Turkey Day!

Shalom, הבת היפה שלי (biti hayafah)!

I'm on the kibbutz, working in the communal garden, picking dates and trying to win the "who can grow the biggest head of cabbage" contest. Honestly, I had it in the bag until one of the Jewish mothers here started giving me a guilt trip about how her daughter would never get married unless she could boast the largest cabbages from which to feed her future children (her words, which I took at face value). I thought it was just social pressure at first, but then I caught her watering my one-square-foot cabbage plot with Manischewitz.

I am coming home, my head hanging in small cabbage shame.

You'd think I would be looking forward to a Thanksgiving feast, but you just could not believe the amount of turkey they eat in Israel. Here I was thinking that I was heading to the Promised Land to enjoy chicken matzoh ball soup. Total myth. It's all made with gobble gobble. Not that it's not good, but it sort of busts that Jewish penicillin image, you know? I can't decide whether this ruins my story for *Food and Wine* or gives me a real scoop.

So, yafah. I *am* looking forward to Thanksgiving dinner, but only for two reasons. One, I just plain can't wait to put my hands on your cheeks and squeeze while I kiss the top of your head. Two, count me intrigued by Connie. Professor Connie Shun. What a yafah name. I am dying to hear — dying, I tell you, like my cabbages — whether she has ever traveled anywhere interesting and, if she has not, whether she dreams of standing on the bow of a ship and holding her arms wide while Celine Dion sings in the background.

Look for me around 7:00 on Thanksgiving morning. Until then, may your cabbages grow large.

Love,

Daddy

Libby shuddered. There was just something NOT RIGHT about her father commenting on the size of her . . . ahem . . . cabbages.

Oh, mother of God. That made her think of something really important.

From: Libby Behl <lbehl@warrenlawschool.edu>
To: Angel Behl <abehl@foodandtravelwriters.com>
Date: November 24, 2014 22:15:34
Re:Re: Ta ra ra Turkey Day!

Shalom, Abba,

If that doesn't mean "father," don't blame me. I can only count on Google Translate for so much.

Listen, you know and I know that you're always up for a good joke. Normally, I'm totally game — you could probably even convince me to hire a Manischewitz hit man to strike back against that cabbage-obsessed Jewish mother. Speaking of whom, her daughter should find a man on her own merits, don't you think? Isn't this like Jacob and Esau? When you lie about your daughter's cabbage-growing abilities, aren't you tricking the groom, who's expecting my large-cabbage-growing hairy Abba under the veil and finds instead pathetic can't-get-a-husband-on-her-own small-cabbage girl?

OK, so on to the purpose of my email. Daddy dearest, you cannot — and I mean cannot — bring up my cabbages at Thanksgiving dinner at Professor Shun's house. First, I mean, she seems to engage in what some might term friendly torture, others just the rite of passage that is law school. I do not need to have her comment on my cabbages in front of the whole class, like, "You aren't studying enough. Look at Ms. Behl. She is working so hard her cabbages are getting HUGE."

No, thanks.

Plus, Anderson is going to be at the dinner. Don't ask how and why grody Harvard Boy is showing up — it's a long story — but just take it at face value that he is totally the type who will laugh about my cabbages to everyone, all the time, over every form of social media he can access and some he can't.

OK, Abba, reply to this email to tell me you got it and aren't already stuffed into an economy seat somewhere over the Dead Sea, ~~dreaming of my professor's cabbages~~.

I did not write that. Lose that image. Forever.

Love,

Libby

•　　　•　　　•

Connie was shuffling around the kitchen, humming the theme from *Titanic*.

Where the blimey did *that* come from? She'd gotten over being head over heels for James about twenty minutes after he'd come out to her, sophomore year. He would be teasing her mercilessly right now. About her sentimentality. And her terrible voice. And her choice of Celine Dion.

Not to mention her butter braised cabbage.

Who the heck made cabbage for Thanksgiving dinner?

She just had to step outside the box. Why couldn't Thanksgiving "fixings" include cabbage? People ate Brussels sprouts all the time now. So butter braised cabbage was just ahead of the trend.

And if her ILT students didn't like it, they could lump it. Along with the lumps that just would not come out of her mashed potatoes.

Felix Frankfurter put his tiny paws up on the kitchen cabinets and sniffed.

"Want some turkey gizzards, boy? I'm boiling them up for you."

She could swear that Felix got a little smile on his face. She put her arms around his middle and picked him up like a baby. She stroked his long tummy. "Your tummy goes on and on," she sang.

Felix shut his eyes and shook his head in disgust. He knew he had an award-winningly long tummy. He didn't need her to croon shlock in his ear to get that.

"All right, down with you, then! Your Auntie Sarah will be here soon. Go get her sofa cushion nice and warm."

Felix ran. His three-inch legs were not ideally constructed for wiener races, but he made the most of them.

Connie wiped her hands on her apron — an apron! James would exclaim. How very Desperate Housewives of you! — and peered into the oven. The turkey looked like it was browning just fine. If the mashed potatoes continued their insistence on lumpiness, she could always say that the menu had been Paleo all along. Butter braised cabbage was so totally Paleo. Wasn't it?

The doorbell rang. Felix turned an about face and ran to the front of the house, barking a high-pitched "bow wow wow" that made the smoke alarm triggered by the buttered braised cabbage sound like Celine Dion.

"Sarah, for the love of God, you're on time. You completely freaked Felix out. He thought you were the UPS man, and I'd already explained to him that UPS doesn't deliver on Thanksgiving Day, so he was ultra pissed off.

"Get in here, girl!"

Sarah stomped her snow boots on the front porch.

"What did you do, custom order Snowmageddon to keep that Harvard Boy away from your turkey and fixings?" Sarah threw her arms around Connie.

Connie made a face at Sarah and peeked out the door. "No JudgeDate. What a shame. And what a shocker."

"He refused to come when he heard that you're notorious for your lumpy mashed potatoes and your weird concepts of 'appropriate' Thanksgiving fare. What's it going to be this year, sister? Last year it was honey-glazed buffalo wings instead of turkey. The year before that it was gravy-stuffed donuts instead of pumpkin pie. James nearly put *you* down the garbage disposal over that one. Even Felix wouldn't touch those groan-uts!"

Both women paused and looked at each other. Sarah scooped up Felix and kissed him on the snout.

"Dude, we gotta help your momma feel OK today. It's her first holiday without James since she was a wee child. I don't even care if she's serving some kind of nasty cabbage instead of roasted Brussels sprouts."

Connie stomped her foot. "Felix, did you tell her?"

Sarah burst out laughing. "I have a nose, Ms. Professor of the Year. I was hoping I was wrong about loading our turkey up with sauerkraut, but . . . as James would say, when you have a choice between eating and starving, see what's in Felix's bowl."

The two old friends were quiet. Connie broke the silence.

"Look, Sarah-belle, I haven't told any of the students about James. And that little future-superstar-in-a-political-slogan-T-shirt is bringing her dad, and I've never even met him before."

"I know when to keep my mouth shut," Sarah agreed. She hugged her friend. Connie could tell she was going to change the subject. Sarah had a number of life philosophies. Today, number nine was going into operation. When you want to prevent your friend from crying over her dead best friend, distract, distract, distract.

"But holy Thanksgiving, girlfriend! Did you say that we were having a real live man at this here table today? As in, a student's dad? Funny how you didn't mention that before. Now, I wonder about the ethics of your snatching him up, given that you have to grade his daughter and all, but unless he's been trafficking cocaine, I don't see why *I* would have a conflict."

Connie looked smug. "Well, his daughter did say he was coming in from overseas for the holiday. You never know what he'll have in his bag."

"As long as he went through customs, I think I can direct his verdict." Sarah headed for the kitchen, Felix click, click, clicking on his too-long toenails right behind. "Now, what needs stirring, what needs basting, and what needs de-lumping? And put a glass of something festive in this here hand right now. You can't possibly expect me to whip your pathetic excuse for mashed potatoes into shape with a clear head."

Celine Dion crooned on and on.

•   •   •

Libby sat in her apartment, looking glumly out the window. It was snowing. No, that couldn't even possibly be the right word for it. It was *dumping*.

No way even her seasoned travel professional of a father was going to make it to Newport in this. However intensely he felt the need to check on her from time to time, he didn't have superhero powers.

She sat down by Breyer's bowl. Breyer swam to the side and puffed his golden cheeks at her.

"Don't you try to comfort me, you poor excuse for a pet, you. You're not even cuddly. And you can't deliver Dad to me. What would John Marshall do? At this point in the day, he's already said he can't rule on the constitutionality of the President's pardoning the turkey. He'd probably demand a good single malt and do shots with John Adams."

Libby jumped at the knock on the door, then walked toward it to peep through the peephole. It couldn't be . . . No planes were landing at any airport within a hundred miles. In no realm of possibility had her dad found a flight.

He hadn't.

It was Anderson, distorted by the one-way glass.

Libby paused for a minute, then unlocked the door.

"Hey, Libby. Happy Thanksgiving. I was thinking we could walk over to Professor Shun's together."

Libby looked at Anderson in disbelief. "You never give up, do you?"

"Nope. I even put on a tie I thought you'd like." Anderson stuck out his chest. Libby laughed. Tiny turkeys ran across the silk, chased by farmers holding axes.

"Come on in, I guess. I was waiting on my dad, but I don't think there's much of a chance that he'll make it here in the snow. Let me grab the puff pastry I made and we can snowshoe our way over there."

Anderson wasn't listening. He was making fishy faces at Breyer. Breyer was sucking face right back.

Libby sighed. The guy would stop at nothing. Seducing a girl's gay goldfish? Now, that had to be crossing some kind of line. Especially when the goldfish insisted he was a) Republican and b) straight. Yeah, right. Even if Breyer found a way to lure Kristin Chenoweth into his bowl, Libby still wasn't going to be convinced.

Libby tied her boots, pulled on her hat, and picked up her tray of puff pastry. "Let's go, lover man. Lord knows that Quinn will be freaking out if we are one six-minute block late."

•   •   •

It was looking like it might be more like two or three six-minute blocks.

Libby was lying face down in the snow. Three dozen puff pastry mini-quiches lay around her. They hadn't even hit the pretty, fluffy new powder. Or landed right-side up. Nope, they were face down in their cheesy goodness in the filthy slush the snowplows had pushed to the curb. The curb over which Libby had just fallen.

Libby started to cry.

"Typical, Libby. Just typical. What were you thinking would happen? Were you seriously deluded enough to imagine that you would show up at your professor's house, with your puff pastries in edible form, with your father on your arm, with your dignity intact? No, that would be too easy. No, instead, you are arriving at a Thanksgiving feast soaking wet, with dirty snow slush down your front, with puff pastry even the professor's dachshund probably won't eat, with the guy you've been trying to avoid all semester."

"Gee, Libby, thanks," Anderson mumbled. "I know that you haven't exactly wanted to go out with me, but that burned." Anderson sighed.

Libby wiped her tears. She looked up at Anderson. The poor guy was standing there with a look that said he'd just found out that Kermit the Frog hadn't scored his own balloon in the Macy's Thanksgiving Day parade this year. Suddenly, her hard outer shell went the way of her dignity.

"You know what? You're right. Give me a hand up. Let's go to this thing together and have a good time. You're a decent guy. Quinn thinks so. The whole section that elected you to the Student Bar Association thinks so. Even my fish thinks so." Libby stuck her hand up out of the snowdrift in Anderson's general direction.

Anderson looked at Libby's mittened hand. He looked at her face. His eyes asked her a silent question. Hers answered.

He pulled her up.

"Let's do this." He brushed the snow off her face with his other hand. Gently.

Libby stood close. She was quiet. She looked Anderson in the eye.

Then, she said it.

"You tell anyone about how I tripped over that curb, you're a dead man. Got it?"

Libby just couldn't bring herself to make the leap and kiss him. Oh, well. That kind of thing only happened in Leonardo DiCaprio movies.

But she was trusting him to keep her secret. That had to be good. She thought.

Still holding hands, mittens to tech-savvy gloves — holy shit!, thought Libby — Anderson and Libby turned down the block and walked through the falling snow to Connie's house.

•   •   •

Connie heard the doorbell ring again just as she was whisking gravy. Gravy whisking was not something you could abandon mid-task. She hollered for Sarah.

"Get that, won't you?"

Sarah picked up her glass of 2001 Pewsey Vale Dry Riesling — among James's many virtues, he had certainly known how to stock a good wine in the house's utility closet — and headed to the door.

A fine looking man with just the right amount of scruff — Latino, maybe? Or Greek? — stood in the snow. A snowmobile driver zoomed off behind him, waving as he went.

"Well, a happy Thanksgiving to *you!* Can I help you with something? Car broken down? Girlfriend lost in a snowdrift?"

"Actually, I'm looking for Professor Connie Shun's house? I was invited for dinner." Angel Behl looked nervous. Sarah smiled to herself. She was going to try to make sure that Connie considered eating this very attractive dinner guest for dinner.

"Oh, my stars above. You must be the dad flying in from parts unknown. I'm the best friend. Come on in."

Felix appeared to have other thoughts. As in, this abominable snowman was not coming in *his* house. Not without a doggy biscuit, he wasn't. He barked "bow wow wow" so loudly that Connie screeched from the kitchen and came out to the foyer.

She stopped. Wow. She had no idea who this guy was, but he could definitely stay for dinner.

"I'm Angel Behl. Libby's dad? I'm so sorry to come at what looks like a bad time. I think I missed Libby at her apartment, so I looked up your address, and . . ." Angel thrust a bottle of Zinfandel at Connie.

•   •   •

She was just as Libby had described her.

Petite. Blond. Just a little curvy. He could do without the apron, but hey, Angel had his wardrobe faults, too. And maybe he might go for the sexy homemaker look, if he gave it a minute's thought.

It didn't even take a minute.

Angel was so totally in trouble. Somehow, he'd ended up in the professor's house. That seemed good. Solid. But the professor's best friend was licking her lips over him. The professor was not — or not that he could see, at least. The dog was trying to eat Angel's left testicle. Angel's daughter was nowhere to be seen. Oh, God, she might even be with grody Harvard Boy.

Next thing Angel knew, he'd probably start talking about cabbages.

• • •

Connie recovered more quickly than Angel.

"Come in, come in, Mr. Behl! Your daughter's not here yet, but I'm sure she's on her way." She gestured through the foyer to the living room, where snow was still falling outside the window. She'd put him on the leather couch. She'd offer him a glass of wine. And then she'd go through the archway to the kitchen, close the pocket doors, and have a quick "Holy handsome guy, Batman" exchange with Sarah.

"Call me Angel. Rhymes with hell. One of the only places in the world that holds no interest for me."

Connie smiled to herself, just a little bit, as Angel tried subtly to kick the dachshund that was biting his sensitive . . . area.

"I'm Connie Shun. I'm your daughter's professor for Introduction to Legal Thinking. She's such a pleasure to have in class."

Connie couldn't let the dog do away with what were probably majestic man parts.

"Felix Frankfurter! You bad dog! Leave Angel alone!"

Felix started jumping as high as his miniscule legs would take him, trying to bite Angel in the face. If he couldn't get the balls, he clearly thought, the face would do.

Connie knew all about premises liability. She was pretty sure punitive damages might be available for castration by dachshund. She swooped Felix up.

"Sarah, can you help? Can you put Felix in the kitchen? Angel, I'm truly sorry. Let me make it up to you. A glass of wine? This Zinfandel looks delicious."

•   •   •

Angel had all kinds of ideas about how Connie could make it up to him. He just hoped he'd have the balls — both literally and figuratively, at this point — to follow through with her on that.

But before he could think more about whether his balls were adequate or whether he still needed to work on his cabbage-growing techniques, the doorbell rang again.

This time, Felix howled from the kitchen. Lucky guest on the other side of the door. *His* balls — and his wiener — were safe from the wiener attack.

On the other hand, Angel took that back.

Because when the door opened, there stood grody Harvard Boy. And he was holding Angel's daughter's hand.

Bring on the wiener dog.

•   •   •

"So, I'd like to propose a toast." Sarah raised her glass. "To this lovely gathering. To our hostess, Connie. To these fabulous, up-and-coming law students. And to Angel and Bob, who were nice enough to round out our little Thanksgiving party."

Bob Cerny nodded and smiled, raising his glass. His mustache was full of stuffing crumbs. He looked like Captain Kangaroo. Without the dancing bear. Or the grandfather clock.

Quinn gulped her wine. "Gosh, Professor Shun! This is such an amazing meal! I mean, I can't even believe how long it must have taken you to cook all of this! Turkey! Chestnut stuffing! Silky mashed potatoes! And this cabbage — wow!"

Angel kicked Libby under the table. He started to laugh, silently, biting his lip. He lifted his napkin and pretended to wipe his mouth, but dabbed the tears in the corners of his eyes when no one was looking.

Except Libby.

Libby glared. Her father had better not be about to make any obscene gestures involving large cabbages. She clasped her hands together pointedly, then put them in her lap.

Quinn continued. "And you have a wiener dog! So, I have, like, always loved dachshunds, you know? When I was growing up, we had two of them." Quinn fed Felix a piece of turkey skin under the table. Felix planted himself at her feet.

Connie pretended not to see. Rule #2 that she'd emailed the students: She was going to remain in denial and believe that Felix ate nothing but kibble. As long as no one fed him any cabbage and made him fart all night long while he was stretched out beside her in bed, they should both be fine. "That's so awesome, Quinn! See, I knew there was a woman of substance under all that tap tap tapping."

"Oh, yeah, they're so great. They kept us so entertained, you know? Especially at night. Yeah, around 8:00 every night, it was like some kind of inner alarm went off, and they would chase each other around and wrestle. We used to call that 'Wiener Wars.' My sister and I always said that Wiener Wars was our favorite show.

"And while we watched Wiener Wars, we'd tell them what silly little dachshunds they were, or what naughty little wiener dogs."

Sarah laughed. "Totally with you, Quinn. Our friend James used to egg Felix on and insult him. Felix loved it." The judge stopped when Connie stabbed her in the hand with her fork. It was a forceful stab. Judge Sarah Abernathy could say whatever she wanted in her own courtroom, but not in Connie's dining room.

Quinn took another sip of her Zinfandel. "Anyway, so, my dad had a small business, you know? And he had a website for the business. So when I was, like, nine, I asked him if he knew how to make a website, and he said sure.

"So I told him that I had this great idea. I thought we should make a website, and we should call it mywiener.com. And I told him that we could get people to send in pictures of their wieners, and write little stories about them, and we could post them.

"I just couldn't understand why my dad and my sister were laughing so hard they couldn't even answer. I thought maybe they thought my idea was dumb. So I told them we should make it even better — it could be mynaughtywiener.com.

"We had to have a really uncomfortable conversation that night."

Even Sarah had no idea how to fill the silence after that one. She got up and began to clear the salad plates. Quickly. She made it into the kitchen in thirty seconds flat. From the dining room, the guests could hear wild cackling.

Bob Cerny cracked a grin.

Angel met Connie's eyes meaningfully. Connie nodded. They had to get Quinn out of this one before someone — perhaps a tipsy Anderson — suggested they check out whether mynaughtywiener.com did indeed contain photos of people's wieners and little stories about them.

Connie grasped at the very first straw she could dream up. "So, Angel, you can probably guess how Felix Frankfurter got his name. But I am thinking that there's an even better story behind Miss Liberty Behl's."

Anderson perked up.

Angel grinned. His daughter tapped her teeth in his direction. He had cabbage stuck in the canines on either side. Then she hunkered down. The story always got a good laugh, albeit at her expense, and sometimes she just couldn't take thinking about the drama. Today, though? She was fine with it, if they could all just get through the meal intact. And as long as he didn't tell too much of how the story ended. Christ, she hadn't even thought about warning him not to tell that part.

"Well, you know I'm a travel writer, right? When I was just 23, I was on a press junket to Philadelphia. The city was celebrating the inventions of Benjamin Franklin around the 200th anniversary of his death. In other words, the Philly Visitor's Bureau was trying to get tourists to town during that horrific recession. They would use any excuse to enlist the media to help counter the widespread dismal perception — thanks, Bruce Springsteen — of the streets of Philadelphia.

"My freshly married wife and I hadn't gotten to have a honeymoon, because she'd gotten a call right before our wedding that she'd gotten off the waitlist for a paramedic training class. In New York, when you got the call, you jumped, so she told me we'd have to get all huggy-kissy some other time."

Seriously? Libby shot up her eyebrows at her father. If he embarrassed her in front of her ILT professor, she was going to use turkey skin to lure Felix Frankfurter right into her dad's lap. It would be so easy.

She met his eye. He found his place in the story. "Um, right. So. I brought Maria along on the press trip. We'd figure out all the romantic stuff to do in Philly — that's where the LOVE park is, and Maria really wanted to get our picture taken in front of the pop art sculpture.

"Anyway, we asked the PR folks whether we could go by Independence Mall to see the Liberty Bell — iconic Philly, right? — but for whatever reason, they thought that was a terrible idea. Maybe they didn't want people to know about the crack? That would be typical PR thinking — deny, deny, deny, and rewrite 200 years of American history.

"So, that night, cutie-pie and I decided to sneak out of our hotel and head over to Independence Mall. She had convinced me that a journalist named Behl could hardly pass up a chance to write about the world's most famous bell.

"The stars were out. The snow was falling. The streetlights were shining.

"And we went hopping, the Philadelphia way.

"Next morning, I was off to Tarrytown to write about the Headless Horseman. Maria was heading back to New York to save some kids who fell out of windows and deliver some babies on the side of the

Cross Bronx Expressway. I figured that night in Philadelphia would be but a lovely memory."

Anderson nodded as though he'd been there, done that.

"Next month, I'm in Miami for the Cuban Calle Ocho celebration, and I get a call from my editor. 'Behl,' he says. 'Maria keeps calling here for you. I do not want to know why your wife is so high-maintenance suddenly. I do not want to know what the heck she is screeching about when she keeps yelling "Philadelphia" and "required physical" into my ear. I just want her to get what she needs from you. Got it? Give her what she seeks. Get her off my phone. And then you get your butt to Washington, D.C. There's a Cherry Blossom Queen who's just waiting to be crowned.'

"Now, I was feeling pretty badly that I hadn't given Maria a number in Miami — remember, this was in the days before cell phones. I had thought that it was going to be a 36-hour, in-and-out type of thing, but then I got kind of caught up in the festivities . . . and now Maria, who was normally incredibly chill, had something so urgent going on that I was seriously worried. Especially when my editor said she kept screaming 'Required physical!' What, had she picked up Hepatitis B from a patient or something?

"Yeah, no. When I called her, turned out, life was going to be a tiny bit more complicated than just missing our honeymoon or forgetting to give my wife my hotel phone number. Turned out, she had a little Behl just ring, ring, ringing its way to be born at the end of the year. And she was pissed, man. She was not going to be able to do hazmat training — the FDNY physician wouldn't let her be around any kind of chemicals or dangerous substances. Her chief had refused to sign off on the paperwork that she needed to complete the program, and he'd told her that she probably would have to wait until after the baby was born to apply again.

"She kept saying that she knew that bell was cracked, but she had thought the condom, at least, was intact."

Anderson guffawed. Libby covered her ears. A girl just should not hear about parents and their prophylactics.

Angel leaned back in his chair and beamed at his daughter. "We came to an agreement. If she'd do the pregnant thing, I'd do the primary parent thing, and she could continue with her career in the fire department. And in the middle of a hospital fire drill in upper Manhattan — think a bunch of her cohorts milling around and *loud* bells ringing — Miss Liberty Behl exited her mother's womb and entered my heart.

"Best night of my life. Fire drill and all."

Bob Cerny stroked his mustache, listening. He found a piece of stray stuffing and popped it in his mouth.

Sarah leaned in the doorway between the kitchen and the dining room, drinking her third glass of Zinfandel.

Connie gazed at Angel, riveted. Now, *this* was a man. And one who traveled. Who wouldn't want to wake up next to her every morning. She likey-ed.

"The really great thing was that, once Maria got one look at Libby's face, she was a goner. Everything after that was all about Libby. The guys at the station used to kid her that she was going to run out of room in the lining of her hat if she kept stuffing pictures of her kid in there."

"So why isn't your mom here, Libby?" Quinn asked. "Is she on duty for the holiday or something?"

Angel looked confused. "Libby hasn't told you?"

"Told us what?" Quinn got a sort of excited look on her face. She loved gossip. Maybe Libby's mom had been convicted of taking kickbacks and was in prison. Or she was really a lesbian and had run off with another woman. Or . . .

Libby looked at her father with pleading eyes. Angel shook his head.

"Tell them, Libby. Be proud of your mom. Don't hide it."

The table grew quiet.

Libby started where she always started when her dad made her tell this story.

"My mom was a paramedic with the New York City fire department on 9/11. She wasn't officially on duty that day, but somehow she heard what was going on and went down to the Trade Center. A lot of firefighters and paramedics did that — people think they were calling each other or saw it on TV or something. They always said they had a calling . . . They were called on to help.

"Anyway, my mom's captain said she checked in with him down at the crash sites, then asked how she could help. He told her to attend to the wounded who were being brought out of the buildings, but then several people said that she started going in to help. She ran into the North Tower three times that we know of. According to the survivors, she was like a locomotive. She helped at least six people get out, including one man who had a guide dog named Roselle. Some people who were with Roselle's owner said that my mom had just gone back in to try to help more people when the tower collapsed.

"My dad and I were in London, because I had wanted to see the Changing of the Guard. It was mid-afternoon when we heard what was happening in New York. Daddy didn't want to say that Mom was probably one of the first responders — he just said she wasn't on duty, but we were hearing that it was hard to get through to anyone in New York, and that was probably why she wasn't answering her phone. We didn't talk about the other possibility at all at first — we just sat and watched the TV in our hotel room, looking at the perfect, bluebird day in New York where all of this was happening. But when we saw the towers collapse, we started making phone calls. We called Mom's station, but no one answered. We called a bunch of friends, but calls wouldn't go through. We called the airlines, but flights into the U.S. were grounded for the foreseeable future.

"Finally, the next morning, Dad's editor called him on his cell phone. He'd just heard from the New York Fire Commissioner. No one could find my mom. The last she'd been seen had been when the people with Roselle had spotted her running back into the North

Tower.

"The embassy arranged for us to go back on the first available flight, but that was three days later. At that point, we'd gotten the news that we expected. Mom was presumed dead.

"And that's the story."

There was a moment of stunned silence. Sarah turned and looked at Connie. Connie was the hostess, and the professor. She should know how to respond.

Angel sat quietly, almost meditating in his seat.

And then everyone started talking at once. "Libby, I'm so sorry . . ." "I had no idea . . ." "Your mom was a real hero . . ." "If I can ever do anything to help . . ."

Everyone except Anderson. Anderson put his hand on Libby's knee and squeezed. She placed her hand on his.

And then she moved his hand back to his own lap.

"All, righty then!" Libby rallied. "Great cabbage, Professor Shun! Now, I'm going to clear the table."

Libby stood and started to gather the dinner plates. Anderson followed. He gestured for her to go ahead of him, then followed her into the kitchen. Felix click, click, clicked along. There was still some turkey on those plates.

Anderson bent down to scratch Felix's head. "Hey, Libs," he said softly. "That's some story."

"Yep," she answered, not looking at him. "That's what they all say."

"I can totally relate."

Libby grabbed a dishcloth from the oven door, balled it up in her fist, and swung around to look at Anderson. "Don't *ever* say that you understand, or that you relate, or you know how I feel. Because you don't. And if you try to pretend you do, I'll go to Professor Shun and tell her *you* were the one who didn't know what apartheid was and Quinn just asked to cover your butt."

Anderson looked somber. "OK. Whatever you say. But you should know — my mom was killed in Afghanistan. That's why I live with my

Nana."

Libby dropped the dishtowel. She stared at Anderson. He nodded slowly. Then they stood at the sink, looking out at the snow falling.

Anderson put his arm around Libby's waist. She leaned her head against his shoulder. Holy crap, she'd misjudged Anderson. Maybe she should screw her feminist, defensive, no-man-ever values and see where this could go. Speaking of screwing.

•   •   •

The clattering of dishes behind him, Angel watched them from the kitchen door. For a writer, he was at a loss for words.

Even after Maria's death, he had so much to be thankful for. A challenging career. A wonderful daughter. A new . . . love interest, after all these years?

But tonight, he'd trade it all — OK, maybe not the daughter — if he could keep that grody Harvard Boy away from his Liberty Behl.

•   •   •

After so many years of friendship, Connie and Sarah could work together seamlessly in the kitchen. Sarah wiped down the counters while Connie put leftovers in Tupperware containers. She had to admit it, the cabbage wasn't really worth saving, but Felix would chew her best — OK, her only — Manolos if she tossed the turkey legs.

Sarah took a slug of wine. "Well, now. That Libby Behl has quite a reason for being in law school, huh?"

Connie stopped in the middle of burping a Tupperware lid and leaned on the counter. "I know, right? Who would've known? She seemed really motivated, but I figured that was just her earthy crunchy, feminist, save the world mojo, you know?

"I don't think I've ever had a student with a story like that before.

There was the woman who stood trial for killing her abusive husband, and there was the guy who was suing the state over refusing to accommodate his transgender daughter, but seriously? This one takes the cake.

"She did say on the first day of class that she felt like she had a calling . . ."

Sarah looked at Connie hard. "You going to mother this girl child? If you do, she's going to want to know your story, too."

Connie went back to burping. "We'll see about that. Now stop tossing Felix turkey skin. You're going home tonight, and I'll have to deal with him barfing all over my bed on my own."

"Don't change the subject," Sarah warned. "What're you going to tell her about your own loss?"

"I'm going to be professional," Connie answered without meeting Sarah's eyes.

"Yeah. Professional. You keep using that word. I do not think it means what you think it means."

Connie crammed the last container into the egg storage compartment. She didn't have any eggs. Mashed potatoes sort of worked there. They'd been egg-shaped before they were mashed, anyway.

"I'm turning out the lights and going to bed, Judge. You know the way out."

Connie headed down the hall. Felix looked from Connie to Sarah.

Sarah shook her head. "No, dude, got no more turkey skin for you. And it looks like any discussion with your mamma is over for the night. I'll be seeing you later in the weekend."

She called out. "OK, I'm going!"

No answer.

Sarah sighed. One of these days, Connie was going to have to tell her own story.

Eleven

Connie got out of the shower and looked at herself critically in the mirror. Not bad. The hair was frizzing a little bit, but a minute or two with the flat iron and she should be good to go. She rubbed a little cream into the tiny creases around her eyes, squinted again, and tilted her head. God, her skin looked pale. She needed a splash of color. She'd been fighting the flu. In her weakened state, she'd even decided to let loose and post about it on Facebook.

> You know you are sick — and pathetic — when you literally burst into tears in class because your PowerPoint won't show up on the screen. And you are the professor. In a law school. And there are students present.
> **Liz Murphy Colton, Kim Waters Harmon, Mary Moncrief, and 6 others like this.**

> **Connie Shun:** I have a terrible feeling that my scamblogger moment may be imminent.

Leslie Kaplan: Hey! That just happened to me last night when I was being observed for a promotion. Except I only cried on the inside. Good times.

David Johnson: Even law professors are human — I think.

Connie Shun: The biggest indignity is that my screensaver of Pomeranian puppies would show up, but nope, no Powerpoint. More Pomeranians. Still no PowerPoint. More Pomeranians. Sobs.

Leslie Kaplan: Don't you have a dachshund?

Connie Shun: Leslie, and you ask why I was weeping.

Yvette Zarrow: I think that could be the sweetest scamblogger piece EVER. More Pomeranians!

Sandy Roman: All classroom technology sniggers when it sees me enter the classroom. Ah, that sucker, it says, always a good laugh to ruin her class.

Connie Shun: I do think the students are likely to remember everything we covered in class today. Too bad it was all about Pomeranians.

Thinking back over it, Connie started to feel sick all over again. OK. *Carpe diem.* On a frigid early winter day like this one, when spring was still about a million years off, her bright pink dress would pep her up.

Connie rummaged in the back of the closet, looking for the pop of fuschia among all of the black and grey. There it was. On the floor. Under a couple of sweaters she hadn't been able to find for a while. Covered in red, wiry hair. Terrific. Felix had probably been using it for a nest. Connie turned to look for her little dog, a scowl on her face, but he had mysteriously disappeared. He was way too smart for his own good, that one.

Connie untangled the pink wool from the cashmere pile and smiled. All she needed was a lint brush. The little ribbon detail at the waist of the dress was festive. The hem was a little, shall we say, *jauntier* than she usually wore. The sleeves had a little cut out on the cuff that screamed "style." James had always said this dress was Connie's best weapon against the winter blues.

Connie realized that she hadn't worn this dress since . . . James.

It wasn't quite the experience that it used to be, James zipping her into this dress, both of them flapping their arms and kicking their legs in a "we'll make it spring" ballroom dance, ending in a flourish on the floor where James got down on one knee, pulled out some shoes with a grosgrain bow to match the dress, and played Prince Charming to Connie's Cinderella.

Speaking of zipping. Um. This dress had a zipper up the back. Well, now, wasn't that a great kettle of fish.

Connie could zip the dress up halfway, but then even her longer-than-average simian arms couldn't manage to reach the gold tassel on the end of the zipper to pull it the rest of the way up. Crap.

Felix wandered in, checked out the mood of the room, and then barked at Connie as she hopped around the room, trying to use the mirror above her dresser as a guide to where the tassel was and how to position her arms to grab it. She couldn't . . . quite . . . get it. Felix whined. Connie looked down at him.

"Look, boy, I know you want to go out for a few, but I can't do it half-naked. Get over yourself and help me." Connie tried turning the dress around so the zipper was in the front, pulling it up farther, then rotating the whole thing back. No dice. Now her arms couldn't make it through the sleeves. Felix sat back on his haunches and gave Connie what she could have sworn was a smirk.

"Loverman, if you're trying to tell me that I should have let you eat the groundhog last year so he couldn't do this 'I'm predicting a modern Ice Age' thing to us, it's too late now." Felix gave a little nod. Seriously. He did.

So now Connie was stuck. Most of her other work clothes were either filthy, crumpled so badly that Connie could never get the wrinkles out before the review session she was holding today, or harkening back to 1999. Think peg legs and even some shoulder pads. Connie grimaced. She had to get this dress on. Now.

It was amazing how the little, tiny details magnified the huge gap that was her life without James.

Felix crouched in the corner and looked like he was concentrating. Oh, no. Anything but that.

"You poop in here and your ass is toast," Connie told him, giving up on the zipper. "I get it. You're not going to help me, but you want me to help you. Fine." Connie grabbed her parka off the chair at her desk and put it on over the dress, hiding the naked part of her back that was covered only by a camisole. "Let's go. Get me your leash. If I can't be fully dressed, at least the accessories will match."

Connie often wondered how it was that Felix spoke English. Wiener dogs were from Bavaria. At the very least, he should bark in German.

But he met her at the front door, his lobster print leash in his mouth, the long lanyard dragging along behind him.

They headed out the door.

They'd only gotten to the edge of the beach when Connie saw a familiar face. Anderson Kraft. Building a wall of stones and shells, fitting them together, one by one.

Could she? Should she? Was there anything wrong with asking a student with a little help?

What the hell. She could be professional about it.

"Hey, Mr. Kraft, what you doing out here in this cold?"

"Hey, Professor Shun!" Anderson seemed to be doing his best Eddie Haskell imitation. "The chilly air clears my head."

Felix growled at the student, leaning his head forward over his front legs as if he was about to pounce.

"Hey, um, dog, please don't go after me, OK?" Kraft took two steps back.

Connie took a deep breath. Crap. She'd rather have anyone but a student help her out. It went along with her wanting to keep her personal life and professional life private. But OK. She was in a bind, Kraft was here, and it wasn't like he could *see* anything. She had on a camisole under the dress. "Mr. Kraft, could you help me with something?"

Kraft looked wary. "Well, Professor, I have to admit that I'm not much of a dog person . . ."

Connie was confused. Then she got it. No, she didn't need assistance with her spoiled prince of a dog. It was the dress, and the zipper, and the tassel that were making her day way too complicated.

"No, actually, it's just that — well, I can't get the zipper all the way up on my dress. Any chance you'd just pull it the rest of the way up?"

"Oh. Sure. I do that for my Nana all the time. Lemme see."

Connie gingerly pulled her coat off her shoulders, exposing only a bit of skin on her upper shoulders. Kraft reached down, pulled up the zipper, and fastened the hook and eye on the top. The whole thing took about nine seconds. Connie breathed a sigh of relief. As she'd been, she would have had to teach an entire class with her coat on. Now she could just be festive and comfy and light.

She belted her parka, then turned around to thank Kraft. He was already gone, strolling down the beach. "Thanks!" Connie yelled. The student waved over his shoulder.

Connie looked down at Felix, who had dug himself a little sand hut and now was lying in it, looking extremely self-satisfied. "Come on, boy. Let's get home. I've got a review session to lead."

•   •   •

Later that night, Libby, Anderson, and Quinn sat around their favorite table at C & B. It was eerily quiet in here. The jukebox was playing old Van Morrison songs. The students drinking at the bar had books open in front of them. Even the waitresses in short skirts seemed to be calling in their orders for potato skins and jalapeno poppers *sotto voce*.

Libby wrapped her WWJD sweatshirt around her shoulders to cover her chest, then unwrapped it again. Anderson tapped his pen against the table to the rhythm of "Tupelo Honey." Not that "Tupelo Honey" had a rhythm. It was getting really annoying, listening to him trying to find one. Libby gave him a look. She was getting an earworm. Too late.

Quinn stared at her computer screen. She typed a word, then backspaced. Typed another word, then backspaced. Then she deleted an entire sentence. She put her head down on the table.

"Quinn? You OK?" Libby put her hand on Quinn's shoulder.

Quinn answered without looking up. "Sure. I'm just trying to finalize my notes from the review session today. And figure out Contracts. Why?"

"It's just that you don't usually like sticky things. Or wet things. Or anything deep fried in lard. And I'm pretty sure that table is covered with all three." Libby looked at Anderson, concern in her eyes.

"I just don't want to deal with Contracts any more. I swear, I don't care whether the goods I buy are conforming. Let them give me a notice of accommodation. Let them say my writing doesn't satisfy the Statute of Frauds. I just want to sit on a beach and drink some rum punch and listen to Luke Bryan sing 'Sorority Girls.' "

Libby grew more alarmed. Something was seriously wrong here. She had to talk Quinn down from the ledge — or the sorority house balcony she was apparently imagining herself on. She whispered in Quinn-speak. "Hey, you. You've been lying there for almost an entire six-minute block."

Quinn sprang up so fast that Libby's beer went flying all over Anderson's pants. He barely even looked up. When the three of them hung out, getting drenched and getting scheduled were just par for the course.

Quinn looked at her spreadsheet for the day. "Well, the good thing is, I can use my last two blocks listening to study group on my way home."

Anderson gave her a look that said he was almost afraid to ask. "Listening to study group?"

Quinn smiled and patted Anderson on the hand, the color slowly creeping back into her face as she got her second wind. "Sure. I tape every session we have. Don't you? It's so helpful to play it back later. And then I can type up everything we said."

It was Libby's turn to put her head down on the table. Anderson joined her. They lay there, surrounded by paper, soaked in spilt beer, Libby trying to think whether she'd ever said anything totally embarrassing. It was almost as if they'd found out that Quinn had made a secret sex tape.

Except, of course, that no one in the study group was having sex.

And they never would be, if Libby had anything to do with it. Really. She meant it.

Anderson started to walk his fingers across the table toward Libby's.

His stealth move was interrupted by Quinn pulling a book out from under his hand. "I can't wait to review what Libby had to say about justice and wardrobe malfunctions," she said. "Maybe it will be on the exam!" Quinn gathered up the rest of her stuff and did a little wave.

Libby and Anderson sat up, watching Quinn head out the door. Libby grabbed Anderson's sweatshirt off the back of his chair. Without thinking, she wiped down her face and hair. She passed it to him. He patted his shirt and the little scruff of a two-day shadow that had appeared on his face.

Anderson handed Libby her Diet Coke. He took a swig of a Bud Light.

Libby started to take a sip, then stopped and looked at him. Holy hell. They'd got into a routine. They were a well-oiled machine.

Her father would say that they were . . . don't think it, Libby . . .

Like an old married couple.

Libby instinctively reacted against the thought. She was never getting married. A woman needed a man like a fish needed a bicycle. But then she slowed down.

Law school was about learning, about growing as a person, about changing your ideas. And Libby thought that she was really starting to change her ideas about Anderson.

The song on the jukebox changed over. To "Crazy Love."

•   •   •

Three hours later, Libby and Anderson were sitting on the floor of Libby's apartment.

On the walk home, Libby had gotten the whole story about Anderson's mom out of him. She understood why he hadn't wanted to talk about it before — telling the stories made it all come flooding back. Been there, done that. But tonight, he'd said he'd really like to tell her about it, as long as she'd keep it to herself. It was kind of eerie, how similar his story was to hers. His mom had been an army nurse, and she'd rushed into a minefield to help a wounded soldier, even though her commander had ordered her to stay put. Three soldiers were injured trying to recover her body. Anderson was going to law school with the survivor benefits he'd gotten from the military.

Anderson had looked kind of nervous when he'd been talking about it. Libby made a decision as they walked into her apartment: She was going to lighten the mood. She speed-dialed the pizza place down the road and ordered two large pies.

"Breyer, stop giving me that evil stare," Libby called out. "I'm sorry I was an hour late getting home to give you your flakes. Anderson and I were reviewing the enumerated powers. And you, fish of mine, do not have any power — not under Article II of the United States Constitution, not under maritime law, not even under Breyer 'El Presidente for Life' executive order — to make me feed you at exactly 9:00 p.m."

Breyer swam around the bowl and waved a fin at Anderson.

"Look, dude," Anderson said, picking up on Libby's efforts to shake it off. "I told her we should leave the bar. I told her I wanted to head back to her place. But when you tell a girl you want to head back to her place, it can be hard to convince her that it's either to a) study Constitutional Law or b) feed her fish. If you know what I mean."

Libby could swear that Breyer nodded.

She looked at Anderson.

"He doesn't know," she said. "He's celibate. Actually, I think he's gay . . ."

"You know why it's hard to convince the girl?" Anderson interrupted.

Libby was quiet for a beat. She looked at Anderson, spread out on the carpet with his hands behind his head.

"OK. I'll bite. Why?"

"Because the guy isn't trying to get the girl back to her apartment to study Constitutional Law or feed the fish."

Libby did not answer. Anderson held her gaze. He reached to where she was sitting.

"Come down here with me."

Libby did not move.

But then she took his hand.

And then the doorbell rang.

"Saved by the bell!" Libby blurted. She stood up, tucked in her shirt, and unlocked the apartment door to meet the pizza man on the street below.

• • •

Connie had been waiting for Sarah in "their" booth at C & B for what seemed like hours. She'd twisted three straws and shredded five napkins into cute little wiener dog models, but she was starting to get frustrated.

Where r u? she texted.

Hold ur horses. On my way, her phone beeped back.

Connie sighed. She hadn't wanted to come out in the first place. There was something sad about the university side of town when all the students were off studying for midterms. It was good that they discovered the large building full of books called a library. She knew that. And it made her life easier that she didn't have to worry — much — about running into them at C & B.

Still, students transformed a campus and its surrounding neighborhoods from an empty egg carton, its compartments just begging to be filled into a jewel box.

Connie played on her phone, checking Facebook. She'd gotten a lot of comments on today's status update.

Connie Shun is reflecting on how to make Monday fun: Come to work in a dress, but realize when parking on the roof of the parking garage at school that it is freezing out. Open email, find out that everything at the LOFT down the street is under $50, today only. Walk to the LOFT when it opens (freezing in dress), buy cute cords, long-sleeved T, new boots, crazy fun fur vest, and necklace. Change in fitting room. Feel stylish and pumped.

Bob Cerny: Ah, so that's the vision I saw walking down the hall on the second floor. Purple fur. Nice. Maybe I'll dye my mustache to match.

> **Sarah Abernathy:** Felix is going to kill you, you know. Fur is *his* thing.

> **Angel Behl:** Maybe I'll have to come back to Newport to see you in all your glory.

Wow. Angel wanted to see her. In all her glory. Connie didn't even want to start thinking about what that might mean. Or about Bob Cerny sporting a purple mustache. She waved to the bartender and pointed at her glass. Might as well have another Cosmopolitan.

The juke box started to play "Brown Eyed Girl."

The door crashed open, and Sarah came giggling in.

"I can't believe you waited this long! It must be close to 11:00!"

Connie raised her eyebrows. "I can't believe you're this late! Where have you been? Or should I ask 'with whom?' "

"Don't ask. Let's just say that I now know why all those defendants in my courtroom get themselves in trouble. Temptation's a bitch." Sarah giggled again.

"I'm going to assume you're joking," Connie answered, not laughing at all. She looked at Sarah more closely.

"Don't you worry your pretty blond head about it, Professor. All legal. Very legal. Although maybe having that much fun shouldn't be." Sarah lifted a finger to the waitress and motioned that she'd have what Connie was having.

Connie sighed and leaned back in the booth. "It feels like Thanksgiving was a year ago. I've got to start my holiday shopping. What do you get a wiener dog who has everything?"

Sarah smiled and picked up one of Connie's tiny models. "He does, doesn't he? I'm stuck, too. What do you get a nice guy who has everything?"

Connie wrinkled her brow and stuck her finger in Sarah's face. "What guy? And don't give me any of that JudgeDate crap. I'm not buying it."

"Just a guy. A sort of cute one. And kind of funny. Sort of like Angel. Speaking of Angel, have you heard from him?"

"Just a Facebook reply. Nothing else. He's probably parading with penguins in Antarctica or something. Whatever it is, it's a lot more interesting than getting ready for midterms and writing a law review article about Rawls's theory of justice."

"I wouldn't be so sure. He seemed to find law school pretty darn interesting. Especially when you were talking about it." Sarah gave Connie a knowing look.

Sarah was quiet.

"Yeah. I liked him. He had a certain . . . worldliness, but one that was familiar. I know that sounds completely counterintuitive."

"Like you'd feel at home with him even in an igloo or a yurt." Sarah nodded. She got it.

"Yeah. Like that. Like I always felt with James — but with a little bit of tingle thrown in. That's the problem, right? When your best friend is that fabulous, other guys just don't measure up. Or, if you think they do, they don't think so."

"I'm right there with you, sister." Sarah grinned and picked up the drink that the waitress had just delivered.

"Thanks. You always under— Wait, you're right there with me?"

Sarah smiled. She raised her glass.

"On the tingle part, anyway. Ain't love grand?"

·   ·   ·

The pizza boxes were empty, the grease soaking through to the floor. Breyer had headed to his courthouse lair for a snooze. Libby wished she could join him.

Anderson groaned. "I can't believe I ate the whole thing."

Libby sat back into the sofa. "I think I'm overcompensating. The less prepared for midterms I feel, the more pizza I eat."

They sat quietly, aware of each other's nearness.

Libby started to speak. "Anderson . . ."

Anderson spoke at the same time. "So, Libby . . ."

They laughed. Then they were quiet again.

Anderson was quiet. Libby thought maybe he was waiting to see if she would say anything else. She didn't.

The pause continued. And then he spoke softly, reaching for her hand.

"There are other ways to relieve stress, you know," he said.

Libby said nothing.

"Have I ever told you how attractive I find girls who wear political T-shirts?"

Libby waited. Quinn would call with a frantic question . . . now. Nothing.

Anderson rubbed Libby's hand with his thumb.

Libby closed her eyes and convinced herself to keep waiting. Any minute, her father would send an email from Antarctica with a photo of himself kissing a walrus.

Anderson leaned over to Libby's side of the couch.

Libby waited one more beat. No Facebook updates from college friends. No disciplinarian emails from Dean Cerny. No assignment notifications from Professor Shun.

Why, tonight of all nights, had the rest of the world disappeared?

Anderson whispered in Libby's ear. "They're all leaving us alone. That should tell us something."

And then he kissed her.

Across the street, church bells started to ring.

Twelve

Anderson stretched and yawned, then gave Libby a big grin.

Across the room, Libby was feeding Breyer his breakfast flakes. It was a fine morning. Breyer was a fine fish. Flakes were a fine snack. She threw in a few bloodworms for a treat.

"Man, I feel like a million bucks!" Anderson crowed.

"It was a great night," Libby answered, without meeting his eyes. She pulled her robe more tightly around her. Even after more than a week, she still felt funny waking up with Anderson. She didn't usually — OK, make that never — have guys back to her apartment. And having them sleep over? Libby couldn't believe that she'd really let Anderson talk her into that. Except . . . "I think we're getting the hang of each other. I really liked it when you—"

"No, I meant the midterm. This whole semester, ILT has been kicking my butt. But that midterm rocked. I feel like I just climbed Everest. You inspire me, girlfriend.

"Man, the view from up here is good." Anderson looked suggestively at the slight gap in the front of Libby's robe.

Libby wasn't sure what to think. Was it normal for a guy to spend a passionate night in bed with a woman, then wake up crowing — not about the great sex, but about a great exam? And while he pumped his fist in the air, should she be subtly letting her robe fall even more open, all the better to bring the focus back to the miracle that was their lovemaking?

Libby was outside her comfort zone here. Protests: She knew how to do those. Paint a couple of placards, put your ID and a power bar in your pocket in case you get arrested, blow into a pitch pipe for "We Shall Overcome." Don't wear makeup, but do write the phone number for Legal Aid in permanent marker on your arm. Feel the love and the passion that could only be found — or so Libby had thought until now — in a large group of people who were joining together to make a difference, to satisfy a calling.

But dating? This was a whole different kind of exhilaration. In Libby's limited experience, at least in college, at least with most guys, love took a distant second place to changing the world. The only world Anderson seemed to want to change was one in which Libby was fully clothed.

If you'd asked Libby a couple of months ago, she would have sneered at the thought of being with a guy. Especially one who wore his pink button-downs untucked and his baseball cap backwards. Not to mention one who watched football.

Her father was going to die.

But Libby smiled a little smile — just to herself — whenever she thought of Anderson. And Anderson's hands. And Anderson's lips. And Anderson's . . .

Libby shook herself out of her reverie. Anderson was lying in the bed, his hands behind his head, the sheet just up to his navel. He was watching her. He was leering.

Anderson patted the bed beside him. "Let's celebrate ILT success," he suggested.

Libby looked at the stack of books on her desk. She looked at her laptop.

She looked at Anderson.

She crossed the room, opening her robe as she approached the bed.

Libby was not going to let fear rule her life for one minute longer. You never knew when your life was going to change — or end — forever. *Carpe diem.*

•   •   •

The Crimson & Blue was hopping, the jukebox playing a party mix leading off with the Black Eyed Peas singing about what a great night it was gonna be.

Midterms were over.

If Quinn hadn't gotten there early to claim them a table, they probably wouldn't even have been able to find a space to stand. But you could always count on Quinn. Thoughtful? Not really. Brilliant? Not so much. Reliable? Oh, yeah. "Reliable" was Quinn's middle name. Just call her "Old Faithful."

Libby had insisted that Anderson go meet Quinn before she did. She'd meet up with him in fifteen minutes or so. Anderson had smirked at her and said, "So, girlfriend, you're not scared of getting arrested, but you're scared to get up close and personal in front of Quinn?"

Libby wasn't sure. She wasn't sure whether she was scared of Quinn seeing them together. She also wasn't sure what exactly Anderson meant by "girlfriend."

Ugh. Protesting was so much easier than this. So was keeping her distance from anything with a penis. A good reason to have a male fish for a pet. No penis. She'd researched it online to be sure.

Libby had pushed her way through the crowd, waving at Kevin Matthews and Ms. Jackson (what was her first name, Libby wondered?) to find Quinn and Anderson raising glasses and clinking. The table was big enough for at least four, five if you squeezed a bit. Quinn was standing right next to Anderson, practically rubbing up against him. When she spotted Libby approaching, she jumped a couple of steps to the side.

"Hey, you two," Libby said. Actually, she wasn't sure what to say. This was sort of her debut as Anderson's girlfriend, and Quinn was getting all sucky face with him? Libby wasn't ever really what you'd call cool. She was used to that. But she was definitely uncool with this situation.

She decided to deflect and break the ice by laughing.

"Did you two see Dean Cerny's latest?"

Quinn and Anderson shook their heads. Anderson picked up his iPhone from the table. Quinn rummaged in her purse for hers.

Libby pulled it up and started to read.

From: Bob Cerny, Dean of Students
       <bcerny@warrenlawschool.edu>
To: All Students
       < law-students-l@lists.warrenlawschool.edu>
Date: December 12, 2014 17:56:12
Re: Beer for brains?

Students:

While you all should realize that you go to one of the most stu-dent-friendly law schools in the country, I still find it a little hard to believe that students seeing cases of beer (under a table in the 3rd floor gallery — waiting to be served at an event later in the day) with a note stating "For Students Please Take" would actually believe the note was genuine and act upon it. Bottom line, no matter how much credit I may give our students for not being naïve, someone created such a note and others followed the direction.

There is now less beer for the 1L "You Climbed the Mountain and Saw the View from the Top" cocktail party. If you have any of the beer, please return it to my office immediately and there will be no repercussions. Or not many. OK, I will not kick you out of law school, but I may kick your beer butt.

I would also greatly appreciate the person who wrote the note coming to see me to discuss, among other things, the line between a joke and good old fashioned stupidity. As you know, I have a fine sense of humor, and I know when to use it. The conversation the note author and I will have will not be funny, but it will go much better if the author of the note comes to see me voluntarily, rather than forcing me to track him or her down. Believe me. You do not want me tracking you. It will not be your idea of a good time. Even if you're full of my beer.

I'm seriously tempted to cancel the party, but I'm not going to punish the students who went to C & B for their post-midterm beers instead of lifting it from the event room. I'll tell you, though, I'm going to mull over the wisdom of holding future events to celebrate 1L milestones. I will leave a town hall discussion, however, to another day when I have hopefully regained my normal sunny disposition.

Dean Bob Cerny

Libby and Quinn hooted. Cerny sounded pissed — and not from drinking beer. Anderson, on the other hand, had a weird look on his face, a cross between smug and sheepish.

"You think I'd better go by his office?" Anderson asked.

Quinn and Libby looked at each other. Quinn put her hand over her mouth. Libby used her hand to swat Anderson across the back of the head.

"Seriously?"

"Well, it was just sitting there. It's kind of Cerny's fault for not locking it up, right? I mean, it's the end of midterms. We're all pretty nuts. So what did he think would happen?"

"Apparently he thought that we'd wait until the cocktail party to drink the beer," Libby said.

Quinn giggled. "I'm with Anderson. Twenty cases of beer? Unguarded? I don't even like beer, but I would have grabbed a cold one."

Libby rolled her eyes. "Quinn, I actually think Anderson wrote the note."

"Hey, no harm, no foul, right? We're here in C & B now, and it sounds like Cerny thinks that's just dandy." Anderson raised his glass.

Quinn joined him.

Libby didn't have a glass yet. But if she did, she wouldn't be raising it. Anderson was crossing a line here.

"Libby, lighten up," Anderson said. He put his arm around her shoulders. "I'm just protesting — protesting school policy about when and where we can drink beer."

Libby kept her shoulders stiff. She didn't want to relax into Anderson's embrace — the guy was being a douche. Did he really think he could bring her around with a transparent argument like "protesting"? She knew what guys were like. She wasn't dumb. Or blinded by love.

Love did make things a little blurry, though.

Libby shrugged. She didn't want Anderson's arm around her, out here in public. But she didn't want to make a scene, either.

And she wasn't actually sure she didn't want Anderson's arm around her in public.

"Anybody want another round?" she asked. "I'm heading up to the bar for a certified, approved pint."

•   •   •

Libby leaned over the fish bowl. After C & B, Quinn had headed home to send her Law Stars instructor an email about her success with his methods. Anderson had gone to meet up with some college friends. He hadn't invited Libby.

That was OK. Breyer was waiting for his flakes.

Actually, it didn't really feel OK.

Libby was worried. She felt like she was falling too hard, too fast. But she couldn't seem to stop herself.

Non-violent protest was supposed to be planned, controlled, right up to getting arrested at the end.

Nothing about being with Anderson seemed planned and controlled.

And then there was law school. Anderson was so sure of himself, confident he'd aced exams. Quinn had never pretended that she was really getting it — but then, Quinn was counting on her Law Stars techniques to get through. But Libby? She thought she'd been understanding it all, but she was pretty certain that she'd missed some major stuff on the exams. She knew she hadn't said enough about "Equal Justice Under Law," just for a start.

This feeling — am I dumb? Am I smart? — it was killing Libby.

And right now, Anderson was the only thing that made it feel better. When he kissed her and told her she was perfect in every way, she almost believed it.

But when he went out with friends and didn't invite her, that *does he like me, or does he not?* feeling killed her, too. Especially because this wasn't her. It wasn't who she'd been raised to be. It wasn't how she envisioned herself. It wasn't the feeling of a daughter whose mother had skipped her honeymoon to do CPR on crash dummies and run into simulated fires.

Life these days felt like a double whammy of a roller coaster.

Libby looked at Breyer, swimming around in his bowl, coming to the surface for a bloodworm or two. He had no cares. He didn't have to worry about acing an exam. He didn't need another fish to complete him.

"It's not fair, Breyer," Libby complained. "I try to just keep swimming, just keep swimming, but it's a lot harder than Pixar animation makes it sound." Breyer made sucky faces at Libby through the glass. "Yeah, I love you, too," Libby replied. "That's why I've kept you around for so long."

Breyer swam in a circle, wagged his back fin, and then settled himself into his courthouse bunker.

Libby got the hint. Breyer was almost as exhausted from this midterms week as she was. And she was pretty sure he didn't like being woken in the night from the sounds of Anderson's . . . passion. Libby, she was more of the quiet sort. Or so she was finding out.

Maybe she'd better fill her dad in on what was going on. She hadn't heard from him in a while — usually a sign that he was hanging out in a Kenyan tribal village or an Alaskan outpost or something.

From: Libby Behl <lbehl@warrenlawschool.edu>
To: Angel Behl <abehl@foodandtravelwriters.com>
Date: December 12, 2014, 22:19:37
Re: Exhilaration

Hey, Dad,

Sorry I haven't really written this week. Midterms have significantly and unreasonably interfered with anything that could conceivably be called a good time. I guess it is foreseeable that I'd go off the grid.

~~Wait, do you think that means that midterms meet the legal definition of a nuisance?~~ Damn it, I feel like I can't even think or write an email without using legalese. At least I crossed it out, right? But that's part of what's kept me from writing to you. I am so unsure about everything here. Everything's a question: Is it a nuisance, or isn't it? Is it constitutional, or isn't it? Is it justice, or isn't it? And I just am not one of those people who has figured out the answers.

Which sort of brings me to the next reason I'm emailing . . . I don't think you're going to like this very much.

I'm kind of dating Anderson.

Actually, I'm dating him for real.

Which is bringing up all kinds of other questions. Why am I dating a frat boy? Who went to Harvard? Who doesn't even know that there was a first wave of feminism, much less a third?

I haven't figured out the answers to those questions either.

The only thing I know is that I really, really like him. And he seems to like me. Even though I'm a nerdy klutz who dreams about stuff like attending a big Supreme Court argument or being a contestant in the National Spelling Bee.

Dad, I know you weren't his hugest fan when you were here at Thanksgiving, but I'm telling you, he's really been changing this year. He's become almost sensitive. Especially since I told him about Mom. That was a good call you made, making me do that.

And how can you not like a guy who loves your fish?

And he gets law school, Dad. He really gets it. He doesn't sweat it. He just figures it out, and he does what he needs to do, and he's fine.

I've really benefited from this way he has of calming me down. I feel . . . exhilarated.

I'm going out now, hoping that I won't hear you screaming at me through the computer.

I love you, Dad. I know it's hard for you to see your little girl growing up. But it had to happen sometime.

Love,

Libby

•   •   •

There was no way Libby was going to pace the floor of her microscopic living room *cum* dining room *cum* kitchen, waiting for her father's response. Whatever he had to say, she didn't think it would be good. Angel was kind of an opinionated sort. Especially when it came to his daughter.

Breyer was no help. He was in fishy dreamland, probably imagining himself a whale or a dolphin. Breyer had a big ego like that.

Libby put on her boots. She was pretty sure some fresh air would help. She unlocked the door, crept out, and closed the door quietly behind her to let Breyer snooze.

It was freezing outside, but in that classic, New England kind of way. She'd been meaning to check out the mansions on the Cliff Walk. They were probably all gussied up for the holidays. It would take a while to walk over there from her student neighborhood, but, hey, the longer she was out, the longer she wouldn't have to read her father's Anderson rant. It was sure to be epic.

Libby strolled along the lighted side of Bellevue Avenue, past the Newport Art Museum and the Tennis Hall of Fame, kicking the snow as she walked and holding onto her keys in her pocket. Carolers sang "Silver Bells" a street or two over.

Making her way through the drifts, Libby wished she had a dog — OK, not really, Breyer was demanding enough — but there was something about an evening walk in the crisp cold that just called out for a furry beast to be wagging his tail and rolling in the snow.

She was standing in front of the Breakers, trying to get her gloves off so she could take a photo of its elegant façade, all dressed up for Christmas, when she heard a "bow wow wow" and then a "Shush, Felix, other people are allowed to walk along *your* Cliff Walk, too."

Libby turned around in recognition. Yep, there he was, the wiener dog who'd stolen her turkey off her plate when she'd gotten up to refill the water pitcher at Thanksgiving. Should she wave? Or should she let Professor Shun have her evening walk in peace?

As it turned out, she didn't have much choice. Felix pulled Connie along, right up to Libby, and barked furiously.

"I'm sorry about that, my dog is sort of territorial . . ." Connie stopped. "Libby! You're out late! Trying to decompress after midterms?"

Libby smiled and crouched down to scratch Felix between the ears. He barked a few more times, then rolled over on his back in the snow so Libby could get his belly. If you can't beat 'em, join 'em, he clearly signaled.

"Yeah, it has been a wild ride," Libby answered. "I'm not sure whether I know more or less than I did four months ago on that first day of class."

Connie paused. She knew exactly where Libby was coming from.

Sarah and James would say she should share.

Oh, why the hell not. After all, at this point she knew this student so well that she called her by her first name outside the law school.

"Yeah, I remember that so well. It's been fifteen years or so for me, but I feel like that first semester was yesterday. I remember tossing and turning in bed, trying to figure out whether I'd mixed up the definitions of 'invitees' and 'licensees' on my Torts exam. And then someone in my section said that they'd written a ton on the fundamental right to travel on the Constitutional Law take-home, and I hadn't even had time to get to that issue, and I was convinced the whole thing was a bust. All I could think was that maybe I should have become a plumber."

Libby started to laugh. "I know, right? And then you can never get the legal analysis out of your mind. The other night, I was trying to kick back, so I pulled up some dumb old movie on, like, USA Network or something. It was about the Olsen twins, who were trying to go to their grandparents' house for Christmas. Their parents were too busy to take them, so they stowed away in the back of a UPS truck, thinking that the UPS driver would eventually wind up in the grandparents' neighborhood. Meanwhile, some thieves came along and stole the UPS truck to get the presents inside. And I wasn't thinking this was the dumbest movie ever produced. I was wondering whether it was kidnapping if the thieves didn't know the twins were back there."

Connie laughed. "I totally relate to where you're coming from. My best friend from college, James, used to beg me to talk about something, anything, other than law school. When we met Sarah — Judge Abernathy now — it got even worse. James would say that we could be eating pizza and playing Monopoly and Sarah and I would start to talk about land use and squatters' rights."

Felix barked and pulled. All of the attention was supposed to be on the wiener dog. Connie looked down at her dachshund. It was a long way down. And he had a gleam in his eye that she didn't like the look of. "OK, boy, I hear you. It's cold and it's snowing and you want to get home and watch Animal Planet. Say goodnight to Libby and we'll get going."

Felix refused to meet Libby's eye.

"That's OK, Felix. I get it. My goldfish, Breyer, is not that fond of strangers, either."

Connie laughed. "You have a goldfish? I love it. Hear that, Felix? Felix is always asking me why goldfish don't have to go out in the yard to poop."

Connie waved at Libby as she half-walked, half-jogged behind Felix down the path. She called out over her shoulder. "Do something fun this weekend! Go bowling! Get a manicure! And don't think once about whether someone was negligent. That's your challenge!" She and Felix disappeared around the corner.

Libby kept walking, more slowly now. The waves crashed against the cliffs. The snow drifted down. From the distance, a choir rehearsing Christmas carols sang through the trees.

For the first time in months — make that years — Libby felt at peace.

•   •   •

Until she unlocked her apartment door, that was. Her computer screen was flashing. Her computer was screaming, "Oyez, oyez." Breyer was swimming around in distress. Libby could have sworn that he propelled himself in the direction of her laptop, then pointed his fin at it to demand that she make it stop.

Either law school was making her crazy, or that fish's brain had grown three sizes in his six years.

Libby locked the door behind her, then crossed to her computer and clicked on the first email. She covered her eyes. Then she peeked through her fingers. She was afraid — make that terrified — to read her father's response.

From: Angel Behl <abehl@foodandtravelwriters.com>
To: Libby Behl <lbehl@warrenlawschool.edu>
Date: December 12, 2014, 23:27:16
Re:Re: Exhilaration

Namaste, Libby!

Your email has reached me in a time of profound peace. Not profound enough that I'm staying off email, as this Buddhist retreat requires, but profound enough that I am not jumping on a plane to strangle that grody Harvard Boy with my bare hands.

Besides, we had to sign a pledge when we checked in here that we would not kill any living creature, including mosquitos. I guess Anderson would qualify as a creature.

Perhaps the red robes they make us wear here are working. And the fact that I have no shoes is also an impediment to my heading straight to the airport in New Delhi.

Well, that just means we'll have to commune with our like minds over email.

One of the things I've learned here, Metta, is that destructive behaviors lead to destructive thoughts which lead to destroyed spirits. We must balance. Yin yang. And all that jazz.

Has it occurred to you that the destructive behavior of allowing yourself to be seduced has led to the destructive thoughts you are having about being too dumb for law school? And that Anderson might be planting these thoughts in your head? I don't want your spirit destroyed, small one. It's far too beautiful.

I'm going to meditate now and wish you peace. But I am pretty sure the yogi here would say you need to chant for a few minutes and then get into savasana. Peace is the true exhilaration.

And if that doesn't work, remember what Ghandi said: "It is unwise to be too sure of one's own wisdom. It is healthy to be reminded that the strongest might weaken and the wisest might err." Maybe you might want to remind Anderson of that.

Your loving Dad

Libby laughed and sighed at the same time. Her dad was nothing if not predictable. When a guy came sniffing around, he was going to use every tool in his parental toolkit to try to get the guy to hit the road — and not the same road Angel was on. But he'd do it with humor, all the better to keep Libby from being offended. And he'd do it from some distant place, making (pretty) sure that Libby couldn't come beat him up for scaring off her ginormous crush.

Usually, Libby got it. She and her dad had always been a team, especially since her mom had died. They were sort of a Ryan and Tatum O'Neal — at least in the *Paper Moon* version, if not anymore — traveling the world together and being each other's best friend. She didn't blame her dad for wanting the very best for her. Even if he had a hard time admitting to himself that "the very best" meant "no boys, ever." A sentiment with which Libby had agreed, up until now.

But this time, Libby was going to have to work on her dad. Anderson was different. He was. Even Breyer said so.

Libby checked her phone. Nope, no good night text. That was OK. She was not going to be high maintenance. She needed space, too. Right. That was what she'd keep telling herself.

She looked out the window at the snow and thought that, if there were any justice in the world, Anderson would call in the morning.

•   •   •

Connie shook off the snow on her front mat and grabbed the towel just inside the door to wipe Felix's feet. The little monster refused to wear even one of the three or four sets of doggie boots she'd gotten him. He'd chewed off the cutest little Red Sox tennies. He apparently felt they weren't dignified, and besides, he had never gotten over Johnny Damon's defection to the Yankees.

She headed inside and tossed her jacket on the armchair by the fireplace. Felix didn't even wait to take off his quilted coat. He trotted over to his blue bed (Thursdays were blue days, Fridays and Saturdays were green, and she could count on a nice steamy pile on the area rug if she forgot to switch the beds out), circled around three times, lay down, and started to snore.

Well, then. The baby was asleep in bed. She could check her email in peace. This called for a glass of wine. James would be rushing to the kitchen drawer for a corkscrew before she could say, "Bottoms up."

She poured more than she probably needed into a crystal goblet James had brought home from an estate sale ("They were giving these away!") and opened her school email account.

No way.

She had an email from Angel.

From: Angel Behl <abehl@foodandtravelwriters.com>
To: Connie T. Shun <cshun@warrenlawschool.edu>
Date: December 12, 2014, 23:31:36
Re: To talk of cabbages and kings

> Connie,
>
> We meditate all day long here. A bunch of the other journalists seem to be well on their way to finding Nirvana, but it just makes me hungry. The deeper into a trance everyone else goes, the more I find myself thinking about your butter braised cabbage.
>
> Well, I guess that's a type of meditation, right?
>
> It's probably not good karma for me to mention this, but my Libby is appearing to me in my dreams. I sense that she is rejecting mindfulness in favor of momentary passion.
>
> Naturally, she hasn't told me this or anything. This is solely a father's deep connection with his daughter's soul.
>
> Oh, screw it (and don't tell the yogi here that I said that). She emailed me tonight that she's practicing tantric yoga positions with that grody Harvard boy. Is this as disturbing to your mental harmony as it is to mine?
>
> Perhaps I'll find peace by remembering your lovely home, your very assertive dog, and your sweet smile.
>
> And I won't mention a thing about your cabbages.
>
> Until next time, I will try to remember the Buddha's words: "Peace comes from within. Do not seek it without."
>
> Angel

Connie took a long sip of wine. And then she took another. And then she walked into the kitchen and poured herself another glass.

Connie seriously didn't want to fall for another guy who was unavailable to her. She'd made that mistake with James. Until he'd come out to her their sophomore year, she'd thought they'd had a real love connection. She'd let the whole world revolve around thoughts of marriage and babies and rocking chairs on a wide front porch. Even after she'd started going out to gay clubs with him and having the time of her life being admired by all his fabulous friends, it had taken time to adjust to the reality that she and James were more like brother and sister. And, to tell the truth, she never really had accepted it. She'd loved him. And she'd never really admitted to him how.

Connie wasn't sure that getting some huge crush on a guy who was never around — who was usually, it seemed, in some distant corner of the globe — was any different.

But at least he was making it very clear from the get go that he was straight. And interested. Maybe she could take baby steps toward seeing whether she was ready for a relationship that could possibly — however unlikely it might be, given his wanderlust and his law student daughter — have a future?

She looked around her lovely home. Her eyes landed on her very assertive dog. She replayed the email in her mind.

And she smiled her sweet smile.

Thirteen

Felix Frankfurter wanted to go out. He paced around the dining room table, whining up at Connie. When she ignored him, he went to the front door and scratched. When Connie still didn't look up, Felix went down the hall to check whether James was there.

He wasn't.

He picked up his favorite toy — a mini Constitution, in ornate calligraphy, with "We the Dachshunds" at the top — and put it next to Connie's chair. He stood on it. It squeaked. He jumped on it. *Squeak squeak squeak*. He bit into it and shook it as hard as he could. *Ssssssqqqqquuuuuueeeeeeaaaaaakkkkkkk.*

Connie jumped. "Dude, you have to stop that. I have to grade. I don't want to, but I have to. By tomorrow at 5:00 p.m. And I still have 37 exams to read. Believe me, I'd rather head out for a walk, too. But it ain't happening. So do I need to put you in your crate?"

Felix scowled at her, turned around, and farted.

"Yep," said Connie. "These exams are stinking up the place. But you need to go hang out until I'm done so we can get them out of here. How's this? Would you like to watch *Lady and the Tramp*? You've always had a thing for that pretty cocker spaniel. And you know what? You can even use your special occasion bed for the afternoon."

Felix cocked his head and ran to the front hall closet. He stopped in front of it and sat. Connie walked over and pulled out a four-poster bed with a canopy and placed it in the small TV room next door. She scrolled through the movies saved to DVR, clicked on Felix's favorite, and patted his head when he jumped onto the bed.

She'd just bought herself ninety minutes of prime grading time.

Connie went into the kitchen and refilled her glass of Diet Coke. She'd gone through a two-liter bottle today alone. By the end of the day, she'd predicted, she'd kill off at least one more. But the soda served three purposes: Drinking so much caffeine kept her awake, holding the glass stretched her hand a different direction from holding a pen, and running to the bathroom gave her a much-needed break every 45 minutes or so.

Connie was nothing if not efficient.

She looked out the window at the mid-January afternoon. Lights were starting to come on around the neighborhood. Smoke curled out of a neighbor's chimney. During this first month of the year, the days were so short that it seemed ridiculous to get dressed. That might be the only good thing about grading. Connie could stay in her pajamas all day long. Even when she went out with Felix, she could just put on her long puffer coat and boots, and no one would know the difference.

James had called these weeks on the calendar the armpit of the year. Even he, usually stylish and upbeat, had spent too many January hours on the couch with Felix, watching *Scooby Doo*, and, when James was in charge of the remote, *Best in Show*. Connie had been in charge of popcorn. Felix and James both demanded extra butter.

Without James, life just didn't have the color that it used to have. But it didn't have some of the angst, either.

OK, then. Connie shook her head, shook out her right hand, and grabbed a pen. She turned over the next exam in the stack. Time to get to work.

•   •   •

In her apartment, Libby was dragging, too, sitting in a baggy "Slutwalk" T-shirt and sweatpants. She knew she should be at the student bookstore, stocking up on casebooks and reading her first assignments for class on Monday. But Monday was still four days away. It couldn't hurt to stay on SCOTUSblog just a little longer. The January docket was full of fascinating cases.

Besides, if she was on her computer, she'd see an email from Anderson as soon as it came in. He had to be back in town soon, right?

Since the end of midterms, Libby had not heard a peep from Anderson. It was frustrating, that was for sure. Actually, it was enraging. They'd had such a connection until the end of the semester. And then he just disappeared into thin air? Even her father never did that. Anderson should know what it was like, not being able to reach someone you cared about.

Maybe Anderson wasn't different. Maybe Libby had been too quick to trust. It wouldn't have been the first time.

Libby looked out the window and debated. If she headed out now, she could get the books she needed. On the other hand, if she snuggled down and relaxed, then got a good night's sleep, she could get up nice and early tomorrow and get a good jump on the day.

Libby went over to Breyer's tank and dropped in a couple of bloodworms. "He'll call tomorrow, right, boy?" she asked. Breyer swam up to the surface. He flicked his tail fin side to side.

"I think you're saying that you don't get what he's up to, either," Libby answered. "This is why protests are better than boys, Breyer. When you go to a protest, you're surprised if anything changes, even if the *status quo* sucks, no matter how hard you try. When you date a boy, you're surprised if things don't change, even if the *status quo* is awesome, and no matter how hard you try."

Breyer ate his bloodworms and swam into his courthouse.

"I'm pretty sure even the Supremes couldn't solve this one," Libby complained. And she went to bed. But not without putting her cell phone on the nightstand beside her, its volume turned up high.

•   •   •

Connie wrapped her arms around herself and shivered. It was getting late. It wasn't really snowing outside, but sort of spitting, sleeting, making a mess that she and Felix would have to trudge through in the morning. Felix was snoring on his canopy bed, his paw on the remote, the final scene of Lady and Tramp with their puppies frozen on the screen.

Connie tiptoed out of the room. She'd leave Felix to his dreams of slurping spaghetti with Madame Pomeranian next door. And she'd grade for just one more hour, get through two more exams, and then head to her own bed to dream her own sweet dreams of spaghetti, soft snow, and a certain world traveler.

Connie sat down in a different chair at the table, this one facing away from the window. Sometimes, just a tiny change of scenery made the misery that was grading just a little more bearable. She picked up the exam on the top of the slowly growing-smaller stack and flipped it over. She started to read. And she started to smile.

Man, reading a great exam brought back that teaching feeling. The one that kept her in this game, year after year. The one that reminded her that teaching was her calling. And this one was the needle in the haystack, the exam that not only synthesized the concepts she'd been teaching in class all semester but introduced some original ideas. In a class of 100, she'd typically see only one or two of these. And when she did, she took notes on the insights, both so she could share them with this year's class and think them over and develop them for next year's.

"I wonder," the exam writer said, "whether law and justice merely intersect or diverge. I think there is a third option, that law leads justice, like when the Civil Rights Act forced America to change for the better. Or, we could ask, does the law change first, or do notions of justice change first? Is there ever a time when the law drives the notion of justice forward, even when people aren't ready?"

The only regret for Connie when she read an exam like this, one that went beyond the classwork into real thinking, was that she wouldn't know for several weeks which student had thought, and thought some more, and written her way into real legal analysis. The policy at Warren Law School was that all exams were graded anonymously. This exam author was only #149946 for now.

Connie scratched a big "A" at the top of the paper and recorded the grade in the spreadsheet she kept open on her laptop. She scanned the column of letter grades. It was the first solid "A" she'd awarded in this class. A couple of A-minuses, sure, and a lot of Bs and B-plusses. Call Connie a hard ass, but she liked to call a spade a spade. If you weren't excellent, you just weren't. No point in telling you that you were a superstar and having you find out down the road, in a law office, that you were comparatively mediocre.

Connie sighed. She reached across the table and grabbed her glass of Diet Coke. And then she flipped over one more exam. It had been a productive day. She was going to sleep so well tonight.

Number 265900. Here went nothing.

Connie started to read. She stopped. She backed up. She read again. Wait, that looked an awful like the sentence she'd just . . .

She put her hand to her head and rubbed. Then she flipped a couple of pages forward.

There it was, on page three. Right where she'd thought she'd see it.

"Is it possible," the third paragraph down on the page asked, "that law and justice do more than intersect and diverge? Because maybe when Congress passes laws, they actually spur justice, and the law ends up leading the way up that path. Or maybe changing concepts of justice push the law forward. Which is it?"

Connie's good mood was suddenly as deflated as a June bug on the sidewalk after a half-marathon.

•   •   •

Sarah Abernathy was in chambers late, getting ready for a trial about liability in a nightclub fire, when her emailed dinged. It could only be Connie. Her love interest had called an hour ago to tell her good night and to stop working so ridiculously hard.

From: Connie T. Shun <cshun@warrenlawschool.edu>
To: Sarah Abernathy
          <judge_abernathy@rid.uscourts.gov>
Date: January 15, 2015 23:09:07
Re: Tell me why. WHY????

Sarah,

I'm so depressed right now. And, for once, it's not because my students' exams are so horrid that I'm wondering whether teaching can possibly really be my calling.

Nope. This time, two of them are too good. Way too good.

As in, one is just as good as the other.

As in, methinks that two of my students have been collaborating. In strict violation of the course rules. The rules that are in writing, in writing on the course website, on the exam itself, in the Warren Law student handbook.

It crushes my soul, Sarah. Do you ever feel that way? Do you ever see a defendant in front of you and think to yourself, "This is a good kid. What the hell is he doing in my courtroom?"

These kids are good kids, Sarah. But two of them — I'm racking my brain, trying to figure out which ones — have listened to the tiny devils on their shoulders and succumbed. James would call it "that moment you never get back."

And now, if I have anything to do with it, they won't get to end up in this noble profession.

No way am I sleeping well tonight. Felix is going to be pissed.

Damn it. DAMN IT.

Connie

• • •

As the sun started to set over the water and the bitter cold of a January Rhode Island evening kicked in, Anderson walked up and down the beach, stacking stones one on top of another, building a tiny wall. He threw a few of the ones that didn't fit into the water. His favorite view, where the boats were silhouetted against the glowing orange of sunset, was nowhere to be found. Most people stored their boats in winter. It made a gloomy mood that much worse.

Anderson knew that Libby was probably in a foul mood, too, but he was at a loss as to what to do about it. He liked her. He did. But he also knew he was bound to disappoint her. He needed her — God knew, he needed her to get through law school — and he was willing to do what he needed to keep her, but it didn't make him feel very good about himself. This wasn't the same kind of "doing a girl wrong" that he'd been accused of in the past. But his parents probably wouldn't get the difference.

Even Nana would be appalled. His whole life, Nana had been trying not to put him down, the way his parents did, but build him up, quoting Atticus Finch to him by saying, "Before I can live with other folks I've got to live with myself. The one thing that doesn't abide by majority rule is a person's conscience." And here Anderson went again, acting like a bottom feeder without a conscience to be seen.

The good thing was that, as of right now, Nana didn't even know that Libby existed.

As far as Nana knew, when Anderson didn't come home at night, he was pulling all-nighters in the Warren Law library. He wasn't cuddling all night in Libby's bed.

Anderson pitched a few rocks as hard as he could. Maybe if he could hit the West Bay, he'd feel better.

Deep in his heart, Anderson knew he could never throw a rock six miles across the Bay. And even if he did, he wouldn't feel better. Not after the ILT exam. He just hadn't been able to figure that puppy out.

At least Libby didn't know. And if things went his way — and things usually did — she would never find out. Anderson knew that the only chance he had of keeping her onboard was to make her think that he had this in the bag.

That was the best version of "happily ever after" that Anderson could offer.

•   •   •

Connie had not slept all night. For once, it wasn't Felix's fault. True, because she hadn't taken him out right before bed, he'd left a puddle next to the toilet in the bathroom — that wiener dog sure knew how to get a message across — but cleaning up dachshund pee was the least of Connie's problems this morning.

She couldn't tell the world what was going on until she met with the Dean of Students. But she did post on Facebook, right from bed, about her distinct displeasure at facing the day.

> **Connie Shun** is conflicted. I really need to get up and start the coffee and deal with the day's unpleasantness. But a little red wiener dog is curled up against me, so comfortable. Should I lift him up and say, "Sorry"? Or should I take a play from his book and snuggle down?

She'd only gotten one reply.

> **Bob Cerny:** So sad to think that meeting with me is dealing with "the day's unpleasantness." And here I'd been looking forward to it!

No, not at all. It wasn't like meeting with Bob Cerny was unpleasant. She liked the guy. She'd laughed a lot with him at Thanksgiving.

He was great with students. He usually had some weird new facial hair fashion going on (thank God he'd never gone with the purple dye), and Connie and some of the other faculty members occasionally formed a penny pool to predict whether this week's style would be Fu Man Chu or a Stach and Patch. Honestly, for an administrator, Bob Cerny was a lot of fun.

But, seriously, she'd rather eat Felix's kibble for breakfast than file an honor code violation report with the Dean's office.

It wasn't just that narcing on students was a nasty bit of business, although it was. In the one or two other cases Connie had dealt with over the course of her career, Connie had always felt dirtier than Felix did after he'd rolled in a dead horseshoe crab on the beach. Of course, the irony was that it wasn't Connie who should feel dirty. Student cheating was bad enough. Student cheating in law school? In an institution that trained future members of a self-regulating, ethical profession? Ugh. The filth of it gave Connie the shivers.

Connie also just couldn't imagine which of her students would do something like this. She trusted them. She believed in them. She genuinely liked them. Some of her colleagues were always trying to employ sneaky cheating detection techniques, like changing the order of the questions on every other exam copy or running papers through a plagiarism scanning program, but Connie had never seen the point. Almost all of her students were honest. Plus, cheaters gonna cheat.

And, of course, the last and most heinous part of it for Connie was the fact that professors almost never prevailed in these kinds of things. Especially when, like this, the two exams weren't identical, just way too similar for comfort's sake — or coincidence, for that matter. For whatever reasons, honor boards — composed mostly of elected students — were reluctant to put the screws to their classmates. All they seemed to need was the lamest excuse from the dirty rotten scoundrel, and they'd sigh in relief that they didn't have to do their jobs and actually punish anyone.

Connie had an hour before she had to see Bob Cerny. Felix was

curled up in the corner, chewing on something Connie couldn't iden-
tify out of the corner of her eye. Normally, she'd call out to him and
see whether he looked guilty or proud, then decide whether to inter-
vene. But today, she was just too weary. Let him have it, whatever it
was.

She scrolled up and down Facebook idly.

> **Sarah Abernathy** is sixteen days into 2015, still virtuously keep-
> ing her New Year's resolution not to tell anyone what she wears
> underneath her robes.

> **Bob Cerny** is contemplating a soul patch. With a white streak
> running through it.

Connie posted again.

> **Connie Shun** is sad. It's so hard when hopes and expectations
> are dashed.

Connie got up to grab a cup of coffee from the pot she'd brewed in
the kitchen. Felix covered his chew toy with his body. Almost. Sticking
out from under his hind end was a block of the fancy cheese Connie
had bought two days ago to reward herself for getting her grading
done. How Felix — with his three-inch legs and lack of opposable
thumbs — had retrieved it from the refrigerator cheese drawer was a
mystery that Connie was just too weary to ponder.

Oh, well. As long as that completely-exasperating-but-so-damn-
adorable-she-couldn't-help-but-love-him wiener dog didn't have ex-
plosive diarrhea in the house — Felix should know by now that he
was lactose-intolerant — Connie would avert her eyes and pretend
she hadn't seen her $10.99/pound Manchego covered with wiry red
Felix fur. Some battles just weren't worth fighting.

The question was whether these two too-close-for-coincidence exams were one of those battles.

•   •   •

Libby unbuttoned her jacket as she walked into the building. She felt a little light-headed, going from about 13 degrees outside to 74 in the Warren Law Student Commons. Seriously, was this what she spent her money on? A heating system that couldn't be adjusted? Every time she entered the school, she felt like she should be wearing a bikini.

"Oh, yeah? I'd like to see that."

Libby startled out of her trance. "Anderson!"

"Thinking about wearing a bikini to school? I think that would be even better than the Lady Justice toga. And that's saying a lot."

Libby wasn't sure what to say. Had he read her mind? Had she said it out loud? Should she even answer him? After all, she hadn't heard from him in weeks. Didn't he know that she was expecting him to ask her out for New Year's Eve?

Come to think of it, apparently not.

Anderson took a few steps toward Libby. He reached out and tweaked the bill of her baseball cap. "I missed you."

Libby was even more stumped. If he'd missed her, why hadn't he *called* her?

She could swear, men were even more mysterious than the United States Supreme Court. And dangerous. Sometimes.

And yet, she couldn't look away.

Anderson suddenly took a step back and straightened up. "Hey, Professor Shun!" Anderson was looking over Libby's shoulder down the hallway.

Libby grinned, both at seeing her favorite professor and at breaking the tension that was this conversation. "Hi, Professor! Did you have a good holiday?" Libby's face fell when Connie just nodded at the two of them and kept walking down the hall, towards the Dean's office. The professor was holding a stack of papers in her hands. Libby thought she looked pissed.

Libby sighed. She had thought Anderson liked her, but apparently not enough to drink even one wee cup of eggnog with her. She had thought she and Professor Shun had kind of bonded over their mutual obsession with all things legal, but apparently not enough for the professor to wave hello in the law school hallway.

Libby started to tell Anderson that she had to go, but he grabbed her hand when she started to turn away.

"Hey. Really. I missed you. I was sort of in a slump, thinking about how horribly I'd feel if midterms hadn't gone well, but then I realized that was dumb. Because grades don't matter that much to me. But you do. In fact, you're the only thing that matters at this school. In this town, even."

Libby decided not to slap him. Then she decided not to leave. Then she decided to put her coat back on and drag Anderson out of this place, back to her place, where she was pretty sure Breyer was having his morning nap and she and Anderson could have some privacy. And after the privacy, maybe some lunch. And then more privacy.

She'd given Anderson a wink and gotten one arm back in her coat when a loud, squeaky voice filled the hall.

"Anderson! Libby! Can you believe we're back? And can you believe the rumor about someone cheating in ILT? OMG, I wonder who? Don't you? Let's go to Legal Grounds and go down the list of possible suspects!" Quinn gave Libby a little wave, then stood on tiptoes to kiss Anderson's cheek. "Hi, handsome! Did you miss me?"

Libby couldn't wait to hear Anderson's answer.

But he surprised her. He deflected Quinn's overly familiar greeting. "A cheating scandal? Seriously? Like, who would do that? We definitely some caffeine to discuss. Coming, Libby?"

Libby stood her ground. "Actually, I think I'm going back to my apartment. I feel like a nap." She waited to see what Anderson would say.

"OK, well, see you in class on Monday?" Anderson gave Libby a little salute, then pulled Quinn's hair and smirked. "Let's go solve the crime!" Quinn skipped toward the door. Anderson followed. He did not look back.

Not for the first time, Libby thought that there was just no justice in this world. If there were, she'd be able to figure out the rules to catching Anderson and keeping him on the hook.

•   •   •

Connie came back out of the Dean's office, her shoulders slumped. This time, she didn't even acknowledge Libby Behl, much less wave and smile. The professor walked right past the student, pressed the "up" button on the elevator, and entered through the opening doors.

When the door closed, she banged her head against the wall. She kept turning her conversation with Bob Cerny over in her head. He'd pulled up the confidential file that the registrar kept with the students' exam numbers. If Connie was being honest, the student who matched number 265900 was not a shock. But the other one? Connie didn't think she'd been this depressed since a certain night last spring.

She should have learned with the whole James thing — if not well before — that life was full of unpleasant surprises.

Fourteen

Introduction to Legal Thinking was underway, same old crowd, a few empty seats. It happened that way every year. After the first semester, there were always three or four students who decided that this whole law and justice thing just wasn't for them. Off they went, to become historians and mobile phone salesmen and small business owners.

But the ones who chose to stay? Those were the students whose imagination Connie hoped to capture. Usually, she succeeded. The way this semester was starting off, she wasn't so sure.

Connie stood in the front of the room, tossing the clicker from hand to hand. Her file folders sat on the podium in front of her, arranged in order of color, sitting at perfect right angles to the front of the desk. Connie's blond hair was pulled back in a severe bun, her eyeliner dark and fierce. She wore a black suit with pantyhose and high pumps. No jewelry. No scarf. Nothing to break the severity.

When the class hushed as the hands on the large clock at the front turned to 10:00, Connie paused, taking a moment to think. When she spoke, it was in a solemn voice.

"I've been thinking a lot over break about rules, and about when it's OK to break them. And when people break them for no reason. And what we should do when people break rules but there's no way to really do much about it." Connie paused again. "If we can't penalize rule breaking, can justice be done?"

Connie advanced to the first slide, a quote. "The function of education is to teach one to think intensively and to think critically. Intelligence plus character — that is the goal of true education."

"I've been thinking a lot about this quote, especially this week. Let's keep this idea in mind — intelligence plus character — as we explore law and justice today."

Connie clicked to a photo of a young African-American man with a mustache. He was sitting and looking out through some bars, his fingers on his chin in a classic thinking pose.

"Mr. Kraft, do you know who this man was?"

Kraft shook his head. "Not placing him, Professor Shun. Was this in the reading?" He started flipping through his book.

Connie ignored Kraft's question and asked the class. "Who can tell me who this is? Who is this man?"

Mr. Lee, a short, quiet man who sat toward the back, looked around the room and then answered. "It's Martin Luther King, Jr. But I'm not sure why it looks like he's in jail."

Ms. Jackson raised her hand and started to talk. "It was probably after a protest. Dr. King led a lot of civil rights protests in the South. A lot of times, the protestors would end up in jail for their civil disobedience. I went to a program about that yesterday, for his birthday."

Connie nodded. "That's right. And this photo was taken after a big protest in Birmingham. That's when Dr. King wrote one of the most famous letters in modern history, 'Letter from a Birmingham Jail.' "

Connie clicked to the next slide, an image of a newspaper with handwriting in the margins.

"Dr. King started this letter in the margins of a newspaper someone smuggled in to him in jail. It was the only paper he had. And with this letter, he made history.

"As we start the new semester, and as Dr. King's birthday approaches, I want to think some more about the ideas of law and justice. For example, Dr. King says in the letter, 'I had hoped that the white moderate would understand that law and order exist for the purpose of establishing justice.'

"Ms. Behl, do you agree with Dr. King's statement?"

"Well, I think that's the ultimate goal. But I think it's pretty lofty. For example, back when Dr. King was leading protests, they used dogs and fire hoses to maintain law and order. But the law and order they wanted to maintain was segregation. So, no, I don't think they always exist for the purpose of establishing justice." Libby Behl's voice sounded much more confident to Connie than it had back in August. When the school year had started, the student had ended most of her sentences with a question mark. Now Behl seemed to trust her own ideas more. It was exactly the path of development that Connie hoped her students would take.

Connie moved across the row. "Ms. Everly? What do you think?"

Everly looked up from her laptop. She met Connie's eyes with a confused expression. "I'm sorry, Professor Shun — what?"

"That's OK, Ms. Everly. Just remember that in law school it's more important to engage in the discussion than to write down every word."

Everly looked horrified. As in, "This law prof has no idea what she's talking about." She bent her head back down to the keyboard.

Connie took a deep breath and reminded herself that these were just law students. If a few of them lacked insight and development, it was their issue, not hers. There was nothing to get riled up about. She should just focus on what was important. Integrity. Law. Justice.

Figuring out how to make them care about these things.

Connie clicked to the next slide, a quote.

"Let's continue. In the Letter, Dr. King also said, 'One who breaks an unjust law must do so openly, lovingly, and with a willingness to accept the penalty. I submit that an individual who breaks a law that conscience tells him is unjust . . . is in reality expressing the highest respect for law.' Do you agree with Dr. King that it is OK to break unjust laws? And how do we decide which laws are just and which are unjust?"

The woman next to Kraft raised her hand. Connie pointed at her. "Ms. Patel?"

Anjali Patel spoke in a soft voice. Connie liked that. It meant others had to really listen. "I don't think we can. If we encouraged everyone to break the laws because they were unjust, how would we have any justice system at all? I think everyone would just see different laws as unjust and soon we wouldn't have any. We have to rely on the system to bring us justice, not take it into our own hands."

Connie spoke gently. "So, Ms. Patel, you're saying that Martin Luther King was wrong?"

Ms. Patel blushed. "Well, he's right when he says that we have to be willing to accept the penalty if we do break the laws. But I disagree that we show respect for the laws if we break them. That's like saying that we show respect for a dog if we kick it."

Connie waited a beat. "Even if you're being treated like a dog?"

Ms. Patel met Connie's eyes. "Even if. You have to trust that the system will punish the abuser."

Connie nodded slowly. She took her right arm and moved it across the semi-circle of seats. "Anyone want to respond to Ms. Patel?"

Libby Behl raised her hand. "But then how can we ever move society forward if we don't challenge the laws?"

A slight Asian man in the middle row raised his hand. Connie gestured to him to speak. "Mr. Lee?"

"We can challenge them," he said slowly. "But we can't break them. That's why Dr. King's nonviolent protests were so important."

Ms. Patel spoke up. "But Dr. King broke the laws against racial mixing and organizing. He might not have been violent, but he did the wrong thing when he acted illegally."

The class was quiet.

Connie clicked again and brought up a photo of Nazis wearing uniforms with swastikas, goose-stepping and hailing their leader with raised arms.

"Well, let's think about this. Dr. King also said, 'We should never forget that everything Adolf Hitler did in Germany was "legal" and everything the Hungarian freedom fighters did in Hungary was "illegal." It was "illegal" to aid and comfort a Jew in Hitler's Germany.'

"So what do you think? Can we decide what's right and follow our hearts? Or should we follow the rules, even when our hearts tell us the laws are wrong? Should we be, in Dr. King's words, extremists for the preservation of injustice or for the extension of justice?

"Justice is *not* blind. Sure, judges — like my friend Sarah — have to be impartial in how they apply the law. But who writes the law in the first place? Not usually the poor. Not usually the disenfranchised. Not usually the outsiders.

"And so, when it's time for a judge to apply statutes — laws made by elected representatives, most of whom are mainstream and upper middle class — those who are least like the lawmakers are least likely to get justice.

"Ms. Patel and Mr. Lee have given us some important things to think about. We'll talk more next time."

Connie put her clicker down on the podium and started to gather her things. The students had gotten to the crux of the debate in all ways but this: What about breaking laws that were, in the eyes of almost everyone, just?

Could she teach students that justice might require them to at least consider breaking some unjust laws but punish them if they violated hers?

Fifteen

Nine thirty in the morning, and Libby was shaking, looking at her computer screen. Could that possibly be right? She'd gotten two As and an A-minus? No way she'd done that well. The computer software had to be wrong. Especially because she didn't have a grade in the space for ILT.

She'd thought, with the new year, that she'd get law school better. But these grades were just proof that she had no idea what was going on. Just like she'd told the world on Facebook last night.

> **Libby Behl** is stupified. Two women at the library today (I think they were 3Ls) were talking about their church (it sounded like they were both regulars there) and some service they'd attended where the pastor had talked about doing good deeds. They then proceeded to marvel at the lottery winner who gave all of his winnings to charity. "That's dumb," said one. "Yeah," said the other. "What's the point of buying a ticket if you're not even going to keep the money for yourself?" Every day that passes, I swear

> more and more that I just don't get how the people in law school think.

She'd gotten 27 likes. The problem? Given that many of the friends who responded were law students, she wasn't sure that she knew which part of her post they liked.

·　　·　　·

Anderson sat on the deck, huddling under his unwashed blanket and a hat. If he spotted a tugboat before he counted to ten, the online grading software would have a bug. Anderson didn't want to think about what the case might be if the software was working just fine.

If that were true — and it couldn't possibly be — he'd gotten a B and two B-minuses. He didn't understand how that could possibly be right.

As for no grade in ILT? He really didn't want to think about how that might have happened.

Better to look for tugboats. And count to ten. Make that twenty.

·　　·　　·

Libby was still looking at her computer screen, hitting "refresh" to see whether a grade would magically appear in the spot for ILT, when she heard a knock on her door. She jumped at the sound. She wasn't expecting anyone, but it was probably Quinn. Whenever Quinn got excited or insecure or worked up about something, she had this tendency to just appear. With grades out, dollars to donuts Quinn was dying to compare hers to Libby's. But Libby had already decided not to talk about grades. It just seemed unnecessary. The three of them spent way too much time exploring each other's psyches as it was. Libby was starting to ache for a little bit of privacy.

The knock came again.

Libby groaned. "You want to get it, Breyer?"

Breyer played dead, rising to the top of his bowl and floating on his back.

Libby eased herself up from her chair, pulling her old "Dare to Think for Yourself" T-shirt down over her pajama pants. She turned the lock, put her hand on the doorknob, straightened her shoulders, and promised herself she would not let Quinn get to her. Libby's grades were none of Quinn's business. Even if Quinn thought they were.

One more knock, this one more like a pounding. "Libby, are you in there?"

Breyer started swimming around in distress. Libby threw the door open. "Anderson! What are you doing here?"

"You see grades were up?"

"Yeah, I was just looking." Libby stared at Anderson. His eyes were red. He had bags under his eyes. "You OK?"

"Of course, fine. I was just worried you might be upset about grades, so I figured I'd come over. Did you do OK?"

"Um. Yeah. I'm fine! I just think it's a bad idea to talk about grades, you know?"

Anderson smiled at Libby and stepped close. "Just between us. You're the only person I want to tell." He stroked Libby's hair. Libby winced. She wished she'd washed it this morning. Or yesterday morning. Or . . .

"It's just that . . . I don't know. I would feel weird about having grades between us, you know? Like, what if one of us did better than the other? And then we were competing or something?"

Anderson touched Libby's lips. "Shhh. It would never be a problem. Not between us. And we know we're not competing with Quinn, right?"

Libby didn't want to ask. She felt weird about it, now that she'd taken a stand about preserving her own privacy. But curiosity was a dangerous beast. And some part of Libby — the part she wasn't proud of — did want to have done better than Quinn.

Anderson continued. "She totally tanked. As in, she didn't get above a C in anything. I think she even got one D, but she wouldn't admit it."

Libby held back a small grin. "Poor Quinn. She must be flipping out."

Anderson looked at Libby hard. "Right, Libby. Come on. We both know that it's pretty satisfying to have kicked butt on exams."

Libby didn't like how Anderson could sometimes see right through her. Like how he knew that she'd done well. And he'd intuited the *schadenfreude* she was feeling over Quinn. And he recognized that right now she really wanted him to . . .

Anderson pulled Libby to him and kissed her.

As they tumbled onto the bed, Breyer swam into his lair. This, he did not want to see.

•   •   •

Connie read the latest email from Bob Cerny, wishing that somehow, some way, something could make her laugh today. Even if this missive, apparently picked up on the law school tabloid "Above the Law," couldn't get her to break out into giggles, it was a relief to know that she'd have some peace and quiet for a while. At least until her next meeting. Make that next *two* meetings. To which she was not looking forward. To say the least.

From: Bob Cerny, Dean of Students
        <bcerny@warrenlawschool.edu>
To: All Students
        <law-students-l@lists.warrenlawschool.edu>
Date: February 9, 2015 10:02:16
Re: I am truly alarmed

Students:

Here's a hypo for you.

First, imagine you live in a world where buildings have emergency exit only doors that have alarms on them.

Second, imagine you go to law school in such a building.

Third, imagine the door has a sign above the push bar that reads in red letters "EMERGENCY EXIT ONLY. PUSH UNTIL ALARM SOUNDS. DOOR CAN BE OPENED IN 15 SECONDS."

Fourth, imagine your professors have offices above the door and that they can hear the alarm.

Here is the question.

When you encounter this hypothetical door do you:

A. Push the door, wait through 15 seconds of alarm while risking annoying your professors, and hope you get out and away without getting caught and disciplined by your Dean of Students?

or

B. Walk around to the front of the building and exit through a non-alarmed door?

Please answer in your head, then conduct yourself accordingly.

And, in the spirit of St. Valentine, please promote peace and love and refrain from alarming me again.

Bob Cerny, Dean of Students

OK, Connie had to admit it. Even in her current mood, she found it pretty damn funny.

Connie dug in her drawer for the Valentine's chocolate hearts she'd picked up at Target. They were kind of melted — no good for reading silly sayings or serving to students — but they went down smooth. And today, Connie needed smooth. A run along the beach with Felix had done nothing to calm her nerves. She'd pretty much not slept since she'd found the close-to-identical exams. Trying to investigate the situation with the help of Bob Cerny, she'd turned this around in her head so many times that she felt upside down and sideways. No getting around it. It was time to do the deed.

A tentative knock sounded on her office door. Connie chewed, swallowed, and choked. She grabbed the Diet Coke on her credenza and gulped. Coughed. Spit in her garbage can. Gagged.

Great. Now she looked sweaty and red instead of porcelain and calm.

Well, there was no easy way through this. She'd might as well look like the mess that this whole situation was.

"Come in," Connie called out, coughing once more.

Libby Behl peeked around the door, questioned Connie with her eyes, and pushed the door open. "Professor, are you all right?"

"Depends on how you're asking the question," Connie answered. "Choking on chocolate? I'll live. On the other hand, I'm not thrilled about having to meet with you under these circumstances."

The student was shuffling around in her backpack for a pen but stopped when Connie spoke. She walked over to the desk and stood in front of the guest chair. "I'm sorry? Professor? I honestly don't know what you mean. Wait, is this about my grade? I tried so hard. I know I didn't really get through all the questions in depth . . ."

Connie felt like her heart was going to burst out of her chest. Shit. Really? She really had to have this conversation?

Here went nothing.

"Libby, yeah, it's sort of about your grade. Do you want to talk to me about what happened with the midterm? I promise, you'll probably feel better if you do."

Libby looked like Felix after he'd chased a cat. Really disappointed. And really desperate.

"I just didn't do a good job of organizing my thoughts. I know it rambled—"

"Libby, that's not what I mean." Connie cut her student off. Time to get to the point.

"Libby, look. Grading exams is the worst part of this job. It's monotonous. It's sometimes depressing. It's, honestly, a major bummer. And that's when everything goes right. When stuff goes wrong, it's beyond miserable."

Libby scrunched up her face as if she were about to cry. "I'm sorry, Professor, I know I let you down . . ."

Connie sat back in her chair. "It would help a lot if you could just tell me why. Then maybe I could help you think about what to do from here."

Libby was using both hands to wipe the tears away. "Honestly, I don't know why my thoughts were so jumbled. I just kept thinking I should keep writing and it would all make sense."

Connie was starting to think that they were having two different conversations. "Libby, the organization was fine. What wasn't fine was the copying."

Libby stared at Connie. "What?"

"The copying, Libby. How did your exam turn out to be incredibly similar to Anderson Kraft's exam?"

Libby hands on the arms of the guest chair started to shake. "I . . . I'm so sorry, Professor. I don't understand."

"You don't understand how I know, or you don't understand what I'm talking about?"

"Um. Honestly, I swear. I have no idea what you're talking about."

Connie leaned forward. "Libby, I need you to realize that this is really serious business. If you know anything, it's much better to tell me. If you lie about it, it can only get worse."

"Professor. I know my exam wasn't great. But I didn't copy Anderson's exam. I didn't! I didn't!" Libby started to sob.

Connie stayed quiet and still. Then she spoke softly. "Libby, look."

Libby looked up through her tears.

Connie placed two exams on the desk, several sentences highlighted. "Look at these exams. Look at how similar they are. Someone copied, Libby."

Snot was starting to run down Libby's face. Connie handed her a tissue. Libby sniffed.

The two women were quiet. Finally, Libby spoke.

"I didn't copy, Professor. That's all I can say."

Connie nodded. "OK, Libby. I understand. I'm going to have to spend some time figuring this out."

Libby nodded and snorted her snot back up into her nose. "I love your class, Professor Shun. I swear. I wouldn't do this."

Connie was silent. How could she respond? True, she'd kind of suspected that this might be the way the conversation would go, but she couldn't make Libby any promises until she'd gotten to the bottom of the whole thing.

She stood up. "OK, Libby. You should know that, until we figure this out, I can't give you a grade in the course. I'll be back in touch, though. You can go. Thanks."

Libby shuffled around, dropping her backpack, then her pen, then her gloves. She bent down to gather them up and banged her head on the desk. More tears erupted.

Libby backed out of the room. "Thank you, um, thanks, Professor Shun."

The door closed.

It was Connie's turn to let loose a few tears.

•   •   •

Anderson Kraft walked down Ayrault Street to the back door of the law school. Professor Shun had sent him an email earlier, asking him to come by her office at 2:00 p.m. She hadn't gone into detail. Anderson was pretty sure that she wasn't about to ask him to be her research assistant.

No, this was not a meeting that Anderson was particularly excited to attend. He just hoped that little pain-in-the-ass dog wouldn't be there. Having to meet with Shun was bad enough. He didn't need an ankle-biter lifting its leg on his good khakis on top of it.

Anderson headed down the hall, got into the elevator, and headed to the fourth floor. When he got off, he could hear what sounded like someone crying. The closer he got to Professor Shun's office, the louder it was.

He stopped in front of her door and knocked. From the hallway, he heard rustling and what sounded like a mother elephant trumpeting. Then there was nothing. And then the professor opened the door.

"Come in, Mr. Kraft." Professor Shun did not meet his eyes. Her shoulders seemed slumped. She gestured toward the chair in front of her desk.

"Professor Shun, can you tell me why I'm here? I promise I haven't yelled at your dog. I haven't even seen your dog."

Professor Shun looked at Anderson for a long time. "No, Mr. Kraft, this isn't about my dog. It's about you. And your ILT midterm."

Anderson started to feel the room spin. He was glad he was sitting down. Whenever he started to feel like this, he always worried that someone else would be able to see.

"Mr. Kraft, do you know what I'm talking about?" Professor Shun sat back in her chair and folded her hands.

"I . . . don't know. Did it not submit correctly on the course website? I did it, I promise I did. Quinn told me she was having some trouble submitting — did that happen to me? I don't want to get penalized for something that wasn't my fault."

"Mr. Kraft, no. Your exam submitted just fine. And you won't be penalized for anything that wasn't your fault."

Anderson was relieved. OK. This he could handle. "Professor Shun, I'm really sorry, but I'm pretty sure that Quinn and I were allowed to talk about the technicalities of how to submit the exam. That doesn't break the honor code or anything."

Professor Shun's voice came out flat and a little bit angry. "No, Mr. Kraft, talking about using the drop box doesn't break the honor code. But copying does."

Anderson felt it then. That strangling feeling. Like he couldn't breathe. Like his heart was going to jump out of his chest. The way it had when he'd had to talk to the college dean about that dumb girl.

"Professor Shun, what are you saying? Are you saying that someone copied from me?"

"Is that what happened, Mr. Kraft?" Connie pulled out the two exams. She pointed to the passage on page three. "Did someone copy this idea from you?"

"Well, I don't know. I mean. I don't think so. I mean. No! How would they do that?"

"Did you copy it from someone else?"

"Copy it from someone else? Like who? I have no idea what you're talking about." Anderson forced himself to breathe, to speak calmly. It was pretty clear that the professor was sizing him up, but Anderson could get through this. He'd done it before. An accusation was just an accusation, unless someone could prove it.

Professor Shun paused and gave Anderson another long look. "Look, Mr. Kraft, I know this is a hard conversation to have. But I need to tell you that I'm not buying this. I do know that copying occurred. If you can tell me what happened, it might be that I can try to help."

Anderson did not flinch. He worked to keep his face neutral. This woman is not a mind reader, he reminded himself. Don't let her try to convince you otherwise.

"I didn't copy, Professor Shun. And I don't know who did."

Professor Shun placed the two exams side by side on the desk, right in front of Anderson.

"OK, well, can you explain how these two exams are so similar, then?"

"The only thing I can think of is that Libby and I studied together, so naturally our exams would be really similar. I mean, we talked all the time about the themes in the course. It was, like, the most interesting thing about fall semester."

Professor Shun nodded slowly. She picked up the exams and put them in her left desk drawer. "So, that's your explanation, then?"

"Yes, Professor Shun. Libby and I would never copy. It's gotta just be that we think the same way after studying together so much." Anderson shrugged his shoulders.

Professor Shun stood. "OK, Mr. Kraft. Thanks for coming in. I'll be in touch."

Anderson stood but did not move from the chair in front of Professor Shun's desk. "What about my grade? When do I find out about that?"

"It won't be for a while, Mr. Kraft. Not until Dean Cerny and I can untangle what happened here."

Anderson clenched his teeth. He did not want to talk back to his professor right now. That would not be a good idea. He turned to leave.

"Thanks, Professor. See you in class."

Anderson exited his professor's office and closed the door. He walked a few feet down the hallway, stopped, looked to make sure the professor hadn't come out, and then leaned his shoulders against the wall. He breathed hard. He looked at his watch.

He wondered how long it would be before Professor Shun was in touch.

•   •   •

Libby stumbled into her apartment, a million questions running through her head. It was impossible that Anderson had copied from her. First, he wouldn't do that to her. Especially not back in December, when they'd been so close. True, it seemed like he'd been withdrawing from her a little bit since exams had ended. But that was natural, right? After the stress of midterms, everyone needed some space. She'd had whole days where she'd just vegged on the couch, Breyer's bowl beside her. The goldfish had insisted that they binge watch a reality TV show about fish tanks. She'd been too exhausted to object, too weary to move except to offer Breyer some bloodworm treats and herself some Cheetos. Then there'd been the day when she'd accidentally mixed them up. Yeah, she didn't like to think about that day.

But the point was, Anderson hadn't had a chance to copy her ILT midterm. She hadn't shown it to him — that was strictly forbidden by the rules. In December, before the exam submission deadline, they'd always been together. After that, they'd basically not been together at all. OK. Not basically. Not at all.

But, those exams looked awfully alike. And one of them had been hers.

Libby locked the door, checked to make sure it had clicked, then sank down onto the couch and pulled the afghan on the back around her shoulders. She had to straighten this out. She just didn't know where to start.

Breyer swam around his bowl, doing laps. One lap. Two. Three.

OK. He had a point. Libby needed a walk. That might clear her head.

•   •   •

Connie hadn't moved from one spot in about half an hour. For all of that time, she had been sitting in her desk chair, spinning a tiny bit from side to side, staring at the ceiling, trying to ascertain just what might help her with this overwhelming feeling of nausea. Even the chocolate hearts, so appetizing before her student meetings, made her want to hurl. Maybe because her own heart was hurting. And not about James, for the first time in almost a year.

Did Anderson Kraft seriously think that Connie became a law professor by being stupid?

There were so many things wrong with that idea that Connie just didn't even know where to start.

Connie coped as she always did these days, now that she could not just head home and spill her fears out to James: She emailed Sarah.

From: Connie T. Shun <cshun@warrenlawschool.edu>
To: Sarah Abernathy
          <judge_abernathy@rid.uscourts.gov>
Date: February 9, 2015 17:13:46
Re: Bells are going off

OK, Your Honor,

Part of your job, I think, is to figure out the credibility of witnesses, and stories, and alibis. Right?

And so I wish you would take over this investigation. I'm pretty sure you'd exclude all of the following as speculation if I were to start arguing it in your court, but let me tell you what I think.

Libby's awesome. She's smart. She's thoughtful. She's interested.

What she's not is very socially sophisticated.

I worried from the beginning that her getting involved with Anderson was going to end badly. It just seemed so weird that a guy like that — Harvard-educated, confident to the point of cocky, Gregory Peck handsome — was going for sweet, smart, kind of shy Libby. She's not a supermodel. She's a real girl next door, to the extent that the girl next door is way into doing social justice. Maybe he likes the fact that she's one degree of separation from a real American hero? But that doesn't seem like Anderson to me. He's someone who's in it for himself, not to admire others.

It's not my place to say anything. I don't even dare tell *you* when you're dating someone less than desirable. How could I interfere with what looks like it might be Libby's first real romance?

And let's not even mention the fact that I have a monster crush — call it wanderlust — on her dad. Talk about conflicts of interest. If he finds out his daughter is in trouble in my class, he'll never like me back.

But, let me tell you, Sarah, as sure as James loved Barbra Streisand, that Anderson Kraft has screwed Ms. Liberty Behl over. He copied her exam. I don't know how, but I do know why. He's just smart enough to know that Libby's the real deal. He scoped her out, he planned his attack, he sweet-talked himself into her life, and then he appropriated her midterm.

And if my gut weren't telling me that, here's how I'd know. When I talked to him, he denied copying from Libby.

But I had never brought up Libby's name.

Oh, yeah, he did it.

So what do I do now? Report them both? I think I have to, right? Because I can't just assume that I'm right and only report him? And should I report either of them? It's not like the Honor Board is going to do anything. The copied language isn't exact. It's too close to be coincidence, but maybe not close enough for a jury of Anderson's peers on the Honor Board to convict him under a "beyond a reasonable doubt" standard.

Should I follow the letter of the law that requires me to report Honor Code violations? Or should I just accept that, no matter what I do, justice probably won't ever be done?

God, I am so glad that most of the time this is not a part of my job. I seriously don't know how you do yours.

Connie

P.S. On the upside, I overhead a student in the elevator today saying, "I stayed home and read the Constitution on Friday night." As I exited on the fourth floor, I told him, "Every law professor dreams that one day she'll be in the elevator and hear a student saying exactly that." I think I'll read the Constitution before bed. Especially the Dormant Commerce Clause. Ha! Get it?

P.P.S. Is it ridiculous to resent Anderson even more because he would have no clue that the Dormant Commerce Clause isn't even explicitly in the Constitution?

Connie pressed "Send" and sat back in her chair again. Time to head home and get herself some wiener dog love. Felix might be demanding and self-centered, but the way that long, wiry body curled up perfectly in her lap? It made everything better.

Sixteen

Anderson was sitting in C & B at the table near the outlets, drinking his second Jager Bomb, trying to work up some liquid courage. No doubt, Libby was about to drop a bomb on him. A bomb as in, you douchebag, I hate your guts, I'm never speaking to you again, and don't you come near me or I'll take out a restraining order.

To tell the truth, he couldn't blame her. That was why, when she'd called earlier in the day, asking to talk to him, he'd suggested that they meet at C & B. He figured she couldn't make too much of a scene in public.

That was all assuming that she wanted to meet because she'd met with Professor Shun. And that Shun had shown Libby the two exams. And that Libby had figured out that the other exam was his.

Crap.

Right before Valentine's Day, too. When he could have sealed the Libby deal with a nice bouquet and kisses in places she couldn't resist.

Anderson signaled to the bartender. He needed a third Jager Bomb. Before his entire life exploded. Might as well go out big.

•   •   •

Libby took a deep breath and squared her shoulders. She needed to deal with this calmly, she thought. If she freaked out on Anderson, she was going to get nowhere. But if she kept her cool, she might find out the truth about what had happened. And then they could figure out a way to fix it.

It sounded like a good plan in theory. The trick was going to be to execute it.

Because Breyer had been signaling to her that drowning was too good for Anderson Kraft.

Libby opened the door and entered C & B, looking around to see whether Anderson had arrived. The smell of buffalo wings filled the air. The jukebox played Fleetwood Mac, a band that apparently thought little lies were sweet. Libby did not agree.

Libby thought that someone in C & B had a sick sense of humor.

Anderson was sitting at a table by himself, drumming his fingers on the table, drinking some weird drink that looked like Red Bull with a shot in it. Great. Hopefully he wasn't too drunk to have a real conversation. Because Libby had plenty to say.

She just wasn't sure how to say it.

On the one hand, Libby was furious. She'd never felt like this, to tell the truth, as betrayed and confused and horrified by someone else's actions. Except when . . . Libby was so not ready to go there. A boy doing you wrong did not equate to terrorism. Even if, in the moment, it felt like he was doing everything possible to terrorize her without figuring out that that was what he was doing.

But there were lots of examples that she could think about without vomiting. There had been that day in 2009 when someone had shot Dr. George Tiller, one of the few abortion providers to help women with fetal anomalies terminate their pregnancies. Just remembering that day, and the candlelight vigil, and the huddling together on the chilly May night with the other protestors — it still made Libby shiver. But as passionately as she cared about choice, she hadn't actually *known* Dr. Tiller.

She hadn't been in love with him.

Christ. Admitting that to herself was hard. She was in love with Anderson. She was in love with a jerk.

"Grody Harvard Boy" didn't go nearly far enough in describing Libby's disgust — and not just for Anderson.

Libby shook her head, trying to help herself think straight. And then she walked over to Anderson. And she picked up the Jager Bomb in front of him. And she threw it in his face.

The shot glass bounced off his nose, leaving a wide red cut on the bridge. The Red Bull in the pint glass ran down from his hair to his collar.

Yeah, all that planning with her goldfish had just gone out the window.

Anderson did not move. He just looked at Libby.

And then, he said the thing it was probably hardest for Libby to hear.

"Libby. I'm so glad to see you. I love you so much. We'll work this out, I promise."

Libby started to cry.

That was right before security arrived to throw them both out.

•   •   •

Back at Libby's apartment, Breyer was hiding in his courthouse. While Libby rummaged around in the bathroom for some gigantic Band-Aids she knew she had from the last disastrous time she'd tried kayaking, Anderson went over to the fishbowl to say hello.

"Libby," he called out. "Are you sure that fish is in here?"

Libby came running out of the bathroom, all nine feet away, holding a bandage the size of a playing card. "What? Breyer? Are you OK?"

A tiny tip of orange tail waved.

Libby sighed in relief, then suppressed a smile. "So, Anderson. Here's the deal. Breyer's not your biggest fan right now. If you want to be pals, you're going to have to work to win back his trust."

"You're trying to tell me that, if I want to take you out for Valentine's, I have to get your goldfish to like me?" Anderson sounded even more stung than he had when the shot glass had hit his nose.

"Pretty much," Libby answered. "We're a team. Like peanut butter and jelly. You get one of us, you get both. And I can't make Breyer hang out with someone he hates." Libby crossed the room to the kitchen to grab Advil out of the junk drawer. Anderson looked into Breyer's bowl and began to speak in a low voice.

"Look, dude, I really like your mom, OK? I promise I didn't copy off of her. We studied together, you know? In fact, she really taught me a lot about that law and justice stuff. That's the only possible way that the exams looked similar. They weren't even the same, just sort of alike.

"I promise, Breyer, I wouldn't diss your mom. She's way too cool. She kind of reminds me of my Nana. She's like a really good tater tot — sort of crispy and tough on the outside, soft and yummy on the inside. She doesn't take any crap. And she stands up for you.

"Any girl who goes out of her way to consider her fish's feelings is the girl for me."

Libby stood stock still in the kitchen. If she didn't rustle around, she could just hear what Anderson was saying. He was trying. He was making friends with her fish.

Who the hell made friends with a fish?

Libby started to relax. Maybe his explanation did make sense. They *had* spent so much time together, it had started to seem like their brains were working as one. There were only so many answers to the essay questions on the exam. Her idea about laws actually furthering social justice couldn't be original, could it? And it wasn't like the sentences on the exam had been exactly alike. None of the parts of the exams that Professor Shun had shown her had been exact copies. There was room for doubt here. Definitely. Boatloads of it. Or fish bowls, at least.

Libby turned around and looked around the pillar that separated her tiny galley kitchen from the living room. Anderson was hunched over, looking inside the bowl. Breyer's body was still inside his courthouse, but his head was poking out, his eyes locked on Anderson's, his head . . . nodding?

Well, that did it. Libby had never known a better judge of character than Breyer. If he was going to forgive Anderson, it was a good sign that she should, too.

Libby shook out two Advil into her hand, tiptoed back into the living room, approached Anderson from behind, and wrapped her arms around his neck. Anderson turned. He gave her a questioning look. And then he kissed her.

Breyer swam back into his lair, wagging his tail fin.

•   •   •

Libby sat up in bed and looked at the clock. 1:13 a.m. Anderson was snoring softly beside her, next to a small streak of blood that had leaked out from under the bandage on his nose onto the pillow. In the dim light coming from the streetlamps outside the window, all seemed quiet in Breyer's bowl.

Libby was alone with her thoughts.

When life was this confusing, it wasn't a great place to be.

Libby eased herself out of bed, being careful not to let the mattress shift. For just a few more minutes, at least, she needed Anderson to stay asleep.

She checked the lock on the door, looked out the window onto the street, and then turned on her laptop and clicked the "mute" key so no random SCOTUSblog on Camera videos would blare out while she emailed her dad.

From: Libby Behl <lbehl@warrenlawschool.edu>
To: Angel Behl <abehl@foodandtravelwriters.com>
Date: February 13, 2015 01:15:56
Re: Law school just does not get easier

Dear Dad,

I really thought that, once midterms were over and I got my grades, I'd feel better about law school.

Deep in my feminist heart, I honestly believed that maybe true love was an answer. Not an answer for everyone. But maybe for me. I never really told you that because of Mom and everything, but honestly I have never been able to really deal with the fact that Mom was working on 9/11 instead of with us. Was that really loving us? I know she did love us, but it's hard.

But the truth is that having midterms over and grades out and a boyfriend who loves me is way more confusing than just plain old fall classes and exam prep and quiet nights with no one but Breyer to adore.

Dad, if I tell you something, will you please promise not to reach a hasty conclusion? Will you just hear me out? Because there's seriously no one else I can talk to about this. If it were something else at law school, I'd probably try and go by Professor Shun's office and talk to her, but this is actually *about* Professor Shun.

And Anderson. OK, so you know I've been dating Anderson. For a couple of months now. And Dad, I know you think he's a grody Harvard boy, but seriously, he's amazing. I'm head over heels. Even Breyer likes him now.

But Professor Shun thinks that Anderson and I cheated on our take-home midterm. She showed me the two exams, and they do look a lot alike. The thing is, I know that I didn't copy from Anderson. So I guess it looks like maybe Anderson copied from me.

The thing is, Dad, there are all kinds of reasons why I don't think that's what happened. How could he have copied from me? I didn't show him my exam. I didn't loan him my laptop. He's never been alone with my stuff, except for a couple of seconds when I ran to use the restroom or to pay the pizza guy or something.

Plus, Anderson pointed out that we studied together, and we got to know each other really well, and so it's logical that our exam answers sound alike.

And one more thing. Anderson loves me.

So how do I get rid of this nagging feeling that won't let me relax and know it's OK and just enjoy being in love? Was this the nagging feeling that Mom had? Is it why she always had to save the world? Because she could never relax and just believe that our family was enough?

You know, Dad, I was hoping that just writing this email would help me figure this whole crazy situation out. You remember how you told me that there are ten little brains in the tips of our fingers? I thought typing out the problem might solve it, too.

Well, as it turns out, I might have a whole bunch of brains. But I only have one heart. And even after writing to you, it's still hurting.

I miss you.

Libby

Libby pressed "Send," then sat and stared at the screen. Maybe her dad was in a totally different time zone, one where it was morning. One where he was sitting in the bright sunshine, his laptop in front of him, open to his email account.

Fifteen minutes passed. The clock glared 1:31 a.m. No answer.

Libby closed her computer slowly, peeked into Breyer's bowl, blew him a kiss, checked the lock on the front door, and walked quietly back to the bed.

She put her arms around Anderson, closed her eyes, and made herself count goldfish. One, two, three . . .

Libby slept.

•   •   •

Several blocks away, in her own quiet apartment, Connie Shun was awake, playing solitaire on her computer. Maybe it was because

Felix was clearly having a dream about bunnies, snorting and paddling his feet and yelping in his sleep. Maybe it was because she'd had too much hot sauce on her tacos with dinner.

But, deep inside, Connie knew that really this was about Libby. And the exam. And the cheating. And how much she wished she could talk to James.

Speaking of talking about it. Connie switched over to email. She was never going to find a red two to put on the black three, anyway. She opened her inbox.

Oh, thank goodness. The first email was from Sarah. Why the hell hadn't she emailed back days ago?

From: Sarah Abernathy
        <judge_abernathy@rid.uscourts.gov>
To: Connie T. Shun <cshun@warrenlawschool.edu>
Date: February 13, 2015 02:02:45
Re:Re: Bells are going off

Connie, my friend,

Sorry it has taken me a few days to get back to you. Had to go down to D.C. for a meeting of federal judges. Speaking of which, if you were sitting in the Supreme Court cafeteria, wouldn't you think you'd overhear all kinds of conversations about law and justice? Nope. Yesterday, while I was drinking a much-needed cup of coffee, a group of elderly women was discussing when they could resume having sex after various surgeries.

Tell me we'll never be those women. At least if we're going to discuss our sex lives, we'll do it in fine drinking establishments like C & B.

OK. As to your dilemma. Yep, you've got yourself a real fine situation here. We judges like to think of it this way.

There's a justice system. It's there to solve our problems. Including credibility problems. And when someone is guilty, the justice system provides for that. The truth comes out.

And when someone is innocent, the system provides for that, too. The truth comes out.

Trust the system. It's a good one.

Off to read the briefs in a huge trial that starts tomorrow. Let me know how it works out.

Your judgely friend,

Sarah

Connie read Sarah's email three times. And then she opened an email to Bob Cerny. She needed to ask him to investigate both Libby and Anderson. After that, the system would do its thing. And Connie would trust it to do the right thing. The truth would come out.

Justice was best accomplished through the law.

Seventeen

Libby woke, stretched, and looked around her tiny apartment. Breyer immediately swam to the top of his bowl, ready for breakfast. If she listened hard, Libby could almost hear his tiny gills breathing out, "Flakes! Flakes!"

It took a second for Libby to remember that she wasn't supposed to be alone.

Anderson was gone.

Breyer flipped and flopped at the top of his tank, doing his best imitation of a spinning dolphin, when Libby saw it. A note. Taped to the bowl. With a heart at the top.

Went for a run, it said. *Heading over to Legal Grounds before class. I'll grab you a coffee. A.*

Libby told herself that it was perfectly normal for a guy to want to go running before class, especially when he had a body like Anderson's. Although where he got the energy after a night like last night was beyond her. Walking approximately nine steps to feed her fish had practically done her in. All Libby wanted to do was drink coffee in bed, and get Breyer to shut up.

But to drink coffee, she'd have to make coffee. Libby assumed that Anderson's offer to buy her a cuppa didn't extend to delivering it to her in bed. Wearing nothing but a barista's apron.

Libby shook her head to clear it. Must. Stop. Thinking. About. Anderson. Naked. She was going to have a serious problem in ILT this morning if she couldn't concentrate. On law, that was.

Libby wandered over to the front door and turned the lock, then tossed some grounds in a filter in her ancient Black & Decker drip coffee maker, poured in water, and sat down to wait. Might as well check email.

Oh, crap. There was an email from her dad. Libby thought back to when she'd emailed him the night before. That was before, before she'd understood Anderson, before she'd figured out what must have happened.

OK. She'd known even before she sent the email that her dad was no big Anderson fan. Or big "guy" fan. Whatever he had to say, she could handle. She could dismiss his concerns. She could explain. No biggie.

Libby double-clicked on the email. A large photo of a man in a grass skirt filled her screen. Then it receded, with words taking its place.

From: Angel Behl <abehl@foodandtravelwriters.com>
To: Libby Behl <lbehl@warrenlawschool.edu>
Date: February 13, 2015 04:09:35
Re:Re: Law school just does not get easier

Dearest one,

Here in Hawaii, I am kaumaha. Sad. Sad. Sad. Even my grass skirt and hula lessons are not helping.

You see, back when you were much younger, I knew there would be times when I wished you had a Betty Crocker kind of mother, one who didn't make it her business to run into burning buildings and stuff. One who would be there for you, and, as you put it, "just believe."

There was the time we were in Kenya on safari and I left the jeep to, shall we say, kick the tires. You were about three, but the guides loved you and pointed out giraffes to you while I, well, watered a bush. You later asked me, "Daddy, I go pee pee out of my bottom, right?" Thinking this might be a question about animals in their habitat or what to do when a warthog appears too interested in human natural functions, I replied, "Yes, darling." You looked at me with those huge brown eyes of yours and asked, "Why do you go pee pee out of your finger?"

Right. You could have used a mother there, at that very moment, for that one.

Then there was the time when you were about thirteen and we were going rafting in Patagonia. We'd gotten through the "Dad, I am bleeding in a strange place" conversation a year or so before — your mom had even talked to me about that one, in the highly theoretical but improbable "if anything ever happens to me" conversation that all emergency responders have with their families. But now we had to have the "you might want to use a tampon and I'll stand outside the bathroom door and talk you through it" conversation. We were doing OK until you asked me exactly which hole was your vagina. Ack. Please give me credit. I did not faint but rather suggested the approximate spot where you might look for said female organ. It worked out fine in the end, as evidenced by your paddling prowess through Class V rapids with nary a leak, neither in the raft nor in your wetsuit.

And now, here we are, in the place I knew we'd someday be, you with your heart broken, me wanting to hunt down grody Harvard Boy and roast him on a stick over a pit. I'd be so kind as to wrap him in banana leaves, but, no, I wouldn't do him any other favors.

If you still had a mother, she'd probably have a much more practical solution. If you had a mother who could "just believe" that love was enough, she might even have an answer for you.

But I'm just a father. And so, my daughter, my kaikamahine, rather than answering your "what do I do" plea, I will share a story, much as the Hawaiians do. Earlier, when I took the attached photo, I tried to video myself telling this tale through hula, but when I tripped over the deck chair outside my room and my grass skirt almost fell off, revealing my "finger," I felt I should do what I do best.

Write.

Last time I was in Hawaii, you were with me, hiking through the Volcano Park and beaching it on the Kona Coast. You must have been about sixteen. You kept telling me that you were getting a yucky feeling from another journalist on the trip, a guy in his fifties who insisted on wearing a Speedo on the beach and shouldn't have. I shrugged it off at the time; we met lots of weirdos around the world, and we usually had a good laugh about them. You and I were always together, so I didn't worry that he could do you any harm.

Well, I was right. He couldn't do you any harm. But you were right, too. He was scuzzy. Remember that, Libby. Your instincts were right. You knew scuzz when you saw it.

It wasn't until a few months after the trip that I realized it. I was on a plane, flipping through one of the big travel glossies, one that paid big bucks and that I'd never managed — at that point, anyway — to break into. I wasn't paying much attention, was just sort of skimming through . . . but then something caught my eye. Some photos. Of a pod of Hawaiian dolphins. That you and I had seen at dawn one morning, all by ourselves, walking on the beach. They were breathtaking.

The photo credit wasn't mine, though. It was Scuzzy Dude's.

At first, I couldn't figure out what might have happened. Could he have been there on the beach that day? Could we have missed him?

But then I remembered. Over dinner the day we spotted the dolphins, we'd been exclaiming about how wonderful they'd been, about how excited we were to show our photos to my editors. Scuzzy dude had said he'd love to see the pictures, but then you were feeling kind of sunburned, and we crashed for the night.

The next day, when we were swimming, I noticed him looking at my laptop when you and I were in the pool. I wasn't crazy about his using it without asking first, but I figured he was just looking at the dolphin photos.

Nope. He wasn't just looking. He was stealing. Loading them onto a USB drive.

I never would have known had I not seen the photos in the magazine. But when I got off the plane, I checked my computer history, and, boom, there it was. "Files transferred" that particular afternoon to an external drive. That wasn't mine.

As it turned out, Scuzzy Dude was super dumb. And maybe insecure. And not just because his Speedo revealed the teensy weensy size of his "finger."

Dumb folks get caught.

'Nuff said.

I'm off to a luau, where I'll toast you with a pineapple smoothie and pretend the pig with an apple in his mouth is Harvard Boy.

You know how to reach me if you need me. I may not be a mother, but I will always be here to sing you lullabies, dry your tears, and watch the dolphin pods with you at dawn.

Aloha,

Your loving dad

Libby couldn't move. She scrolled up and read the email again. Again. Again. Again. The fourth or fifth time, she skipped over the "how could he bring this up ten years later" description of the tampon lesson and just read the part about Scuzzy Dude.

Her dad was right. She knew scuzz when she saw it. She wondered why she'd doubted that about herself. One mistake did not an idiot make.

Not once did she wonder about how Anderson might look in a Speedo.

•   •   •

The sun was starting to go down over Newport, and Libby needed a walk. Come to think of it, she needed a drink. She wasn't in the habit of drinking alone, and she definitely tried to avoid walking alone at night — the last thing she wanted was to have paramedics called out, something her mom had warned her about a lot. But desperate circumstances called for desperate measures. She'd been thinking about Anderson, and computers, and USB drives, and her father, and Scuzzy Dude all day long.

Libby threw on her jacket, braced herself for the frigid February night outside, and checked to make sure Breyer was still napping. If she left without giving him a treat to make the evening pass more quickly, she was likely to come home to one very passive-aggressive fish.

Libby locked the door, went down the stairs, and walked along Kay Street, making her way to the main drag on the edge of campus. The streetlights shone bright. She could hear the music coming from C & B half a block away. Even at 5:00 on a Tuesday evening, the place was hopping.

A sign on the bar's door declared it to be '70s night. Libby wasn't sure what meant, but knowing C & B, it probably involved cheesy music, pigs in blankets, and Slow Comfortable Screws on special. What the hell. A modern girl could get into some tasty rumaki.

Libby opened the door and rubbed her hands together to get her circulation moving. Sure enough, the jukebox was blaring. With ABBA. Who were singing about being cheated by a lover, but forgetting about it in the clutches of passion.

Libby tossed her jacket over the back of a stool, sat down at the bar several stools away from a few guys in baseball caps who were laughing loudly over one who had apparently just puked in the restroom. She ordered a Harvey Wallbanger, not that she had any idea what that was, but the bright orange color seemed cheerful, and hell, they were $2.50. Down the bar, Matthews sat on a high stool, dangling his loafer-clad feet, eating peanuts and chatting with a guy from their section whom Libby didn't know. Matthews raised a glass to her. She smiled, raised hers back, and chugged. And choked. Man, that was awful. Didn't they do Jell-o shots in the '70s? And if so, could she have six or seven now, please?

But even as she drank the last few swallows of the neon orange disaster that was her Happy Hour cocktail, Libby realized that what she was really doing was giving herself liquid courage.

Libby put three dollars on the bar, waved a thanks to the bartender, and pulled her arms through the sleeves of her jacket. She put her hands in the pockets in what was, for her, a particularly determined stance. And then she headed home, walking quickly, looking side to side to make sure she was still alone. It was time to check the cache history on her computer.

•   •   •

Just as Libby turned the corner onto Cranston Avenue, Connie opened the door to C & B. She'd gotten an automated email from the bar's mailing list announcing '70s night, and Connie had headed right out. Felix *loved* sweet and sour meatballs; Connie was pretty sure she could snag a few and put them in her pockets. As for Connie, she was just a fan of sour apple bellinis. Yum.

Connie sat at the bar, sipping the drink the bartender had just delivered, humming along to the jukebox blasting Sara Bareilles singing about being brave, feeling less self-conscious than she usually did when surrounded by students in a social setting. Maybe she was starting to relax. Maybe it was because of the conversation she'd had last week with Sarah, when Connie had been trying to extract information about Sarah's mysterious love interest, and Sarah had been trying to change the subject by bugging Connie to go out to C & B, even though the judge knew it would be full of 1Ls celebrating the end of the week.

Connie had resisted. Students shouldn't see professors with their guards down. Should they? She'd tried to explain.

"You know, even when the whole James thing happened, I didn't tell my students what was going on with me because I thought I shouldn't. I guess I thought that professionalism required me to maintain some kind of distance. I know that my personal life isn't relevant to my students' legal education. Honestly, I think it would be inappropriate to burden my students with my problems."

"OK, but having a drink with a friend isn't a problem. It's a normal part of adult life," Sarah had shot back.

"You know, I'm partly confused about what to disclose to students

— or even let them see — about my own life because they are adults, not children. You know. I'm their professor. I'm still steering the ship, even though I try not to be a 'sage on the stage.' I'm always trying to figure out if the power dynamic means I shouldn't let them see me out drinking at a bar with my best friend.

"So, you know, should I tell them that I went to the Lady Gaga concert when I was in Vegas last spring at that conference? Do I tell them that I lost 30 pounds one summer on Weight Watchers? How about my loyalty to the Red Sox? Should they know about that? Or, that rum and Diet Coke is my favorite drink?

"I know I'm never going to tell them when I have a fight with my mom, or when I wear a glittery miniskirt to the concert, or when I have a best friend crisis, for God's sake.

"But I just never know. Can I let them see me drinking? Or should I just have my nine-hundredth Diet Coke of the day?"

Connie didn't really understand why Sarah was so insistent about this "let them see the real you" thing. The thing was, Sarah was usually right. She hadn't gotten to be a judge for nothing. Even though every cell in Connie's body fought against it, she figured that she could take baby steps to see whether Sarah — and, let's face it, James — had been close to on base. It was sort of a Scout talking to Atticus Finch moment: "Atticus, you must be wrong . . . ." "How's that?" "Well, most folks seem to think they're right and you're wrong . . . ." In the end, Atticus had turned out to be right. Was Sarah right? Who knew?

Connie could not imagine telling students about how her best friend and wannabe lover James had died, and how that had devastated her, and especially how it meant that she'd never know what could have happened between them, even if she really did know.

Nothing. Nothing would have happened. James had been gay. He had loved her. But he had been gay. In fact, if he'd been straight and married to her, he wouldn't have died in the first place.

Connie took a big slurp of her sour apple bellini.

•   •   •

Anderson had gotten the '70s night email from C & B, too, and he was debating on whether to call Libby. She might want to go. On the other hand, she might have thought more about the whole ILT take-home thing and gotten pissed all over again.

He was pondering, about to pick up his phone and send her a text, when he heard a knock on his door. When he opened it and saw who was on the other side, all thoughts of texting Libby went out the window.

Anderson had some bigger fish to fry.

•   •   •

Libby walked into her apartment, locked the door, pulled down the Venetian blinds, and turned on all the lights. She sat down at her desk and looked at her closed laptop. Libby drummed her fingers on the table, beating out a rhythm that eventually she realized was "Mamma Mia." Boy, did those lyrics about guys cheating resonate. At least, she thought they probably did. Well, no, they probably didn't. Anderson wouldn't do that to her, right?

But there was only one way to find out.

She opened her laptop and opened Microsoft Word. She clicked on "File" in the top left hand corner.

When the menu came up, she hesitated.

She heard a splash.

Breyer was diving from the top of his bowl to the bottom.

If Libby hadn't known better, she would have sworn that her gold-fish was telling her to take the plunge.

Alrighty, then. If even her fish thought she was a chicken, it was a sure sign that she should do something about it. Libby had never in her life backed away from a challenge.

She clicked on "Recent."

She scanned the list of documents that came up.

And then she froze. There it was. December 1, 2014.

According to the tracking software her father had installed on this laptop back when it was his, her ILT exam had been opened, then saved to an external drive.

Libby opened a new window and typed a URL into Google Chrome. On the home page for Crazy Dough's, she typed in her username and password. And she waited for her account to come up.

She'd ordered pizza a lot during midterms, but since the New Year, she'd been trying to save both her wallet and her waistline. The last account entries were back in December. One stood out.

She'd ordered two pies — one pepperoni, one vegetarian — and a two-liter bottle of Diet Coke. It had taken a while for them to get to her, and the manager had put a $3.00 credit in her account. When they'd finally arrived, they'd been delivered at 10:29 p.m. On December 1.

Just over an hour later, Anderson had been whispering sweet nothings in her ear.

Libby sat, shell shocked. And then she did the second Google search. She pulled up the *Washington Post's* website, "Faces of the Fallen." She typed "Kraft" into the search box.

Zero results. No one named Kraft had died in either Iraq or Afghanistan.

Libby googled "army nurse killed in mine field Afghanistan." A string of articles from about a year before popped up. The facts were exactly as Anderson had described them.

But all of the stories were about a twenty-five-year-old woman named Jennifer Moreno.

•   •   •

Several hours later, Libby was still sitting in front of her computer, this time reading old Dahlia Lithwick columns on *Slate*. According to Dahlia, the Supremes worried about lying, too, and they'd spent an entire oral argument going through the various permutations in a case about lying about military honors. As the divine Dahlia put it (God, Libby wanted to meet her someday), "At the halftime, we have Kennedy worrying about the truth of falsity, the Chief Justice fretting about academic liars, Ginsburg anxious about Holocaust deniers, Kagan worrying about lying politicians, and Sotomayor panicked about the passel of deceptive bachelors she keeps meeting on eHarmony."

The saddest part about this? The Nine had held that lying — at least about winning military medals — was OK under the First Amendment.

Libby tried to put the Supremes out of her mind. Warren was a private law school, after all, so the First Amendment didn't apply. Maybe Dahlia had written something happier, and Libby could find it if she just kept looking.

Every time Libby had managed to distract herself with thoughts of great things the Supreme Court had done (striking down segregation, for example, and upholding women's rights to access abortion), her mind kept going back and forth to the document history. Usually, a good Dahlia-fest was a tonic for almost anything, but tonight, no matter how many times she prayed to the divine Dahlia, the document history remained the same. Someone — OK, Anderson — had opened her ILT exam. Someone — oh, God, it hurt to say this, *Anderson* — had copied it onto a USB drive. And someone — Libby couldn't get herself to say his name even one more time — had altered the exam just a bit, then handed it in as his own.

The same someone who had stolen the story of a real war hero and appropriated it for his own purposes.

All she needed was for Breyer to start floating on the top of his bowl, and this would officially qualify as the worst night of her life. Well, the second worst. But she wasn't going to go there in her mind right now, or she'd truly go crazy.

"Oyez, oyez."

Libby sighed. Whatever this email was, it had better be good.

From: Bob Cerny, Dean of Students
        <bcerny@warrenlawschool.edu>
To: All Students
        <law-students-l@lists.warrenlawschool.edu>
Date: February 13, 2015 22:56:12
Re: Paraphrasing the Talmud

Dear Students,

Now that I have your attention, the Google machine tells me the phrase "cleanliness is next to godliness," is attributable to "Phineas ben Yair, a rabbi whose writings can be found in the Talmud," where the words "cleanliness" and "godliness" are literally next to each other.

I think my three older sisters used this phrase a lot, along with physical threats, when drilling it into my head that I needed to put down the toilet seat.

So what does this mean to you? Simply put, please make an effort to clean up after yourself in the law school. While we have a janitorial staff, it is not their job to follow you around and clean up after you, any more than it was my sisters' job to mop up after my pee.

Some specific examples include:

- leaving food in the fridges for days or weeks on end (could literally be a stinky, rotten thing to do);

- leaving a water puddle in front of the fridge after getting water (come by my office, and I'll gladly show you the bruise on my butt, which did not come from a beating from my sisters but rather from a not-at-all comical slip and fall when I was merely trying to hydrate, as dictated by my nutritionist);

- stuffing food down the drain that does not have a garbage disposal (you are the disposal and the trash can is the proper receptacle); and

- leaving stuff on top of lockers (yep, bruise on my shoulder, too —see *gravity sucks*).

No one has ever accused me of being godly, but if I can remember to try to be neat and tidy, I bet you can too.

Bob Cerny, Dean of Students

P.S. Don't make me call my sisters!

Libby seriously wished that Bob Cerny, Dean of Students, could clean up the mess she found herself in right now.

Talk about a mess. Libby wondered what would have happened if she'd never told her dad about Anderson and Professor Shun's accusations. Libby could have gone on contentedly, doing her homework, storing it on her computer, grabbing pizza to eat with her boyfriend, and getting scammed. That would have been fine, right? Everyone would have been happy.

Now everyone was miserable. And furious. And maybe even betrayed. Libby most of all.

Oh, wait. Except Anderson. Who presumably believed he was getting away with the whole thing. And who thought he'd successfully picked the most gullible, idiotic girlfriend on the planet. Which he probably had. She'd certainly proven her gullibility in the past. No good could come of that.

Next thing Libby knew, *Dateline* would be doing a special broadcast. This was perfect for that sensationalistic, exploitative, piece-of-crap of a show — a story about the wily, sexy, irresistible playboy and the desperate women he lured right into his trap. Yeah. They'd done that story more than a few times before. Too bad Libby wasn't a regular viewer — maybe she'd have taken heed.

Libby started Googling furiously, looking for information about hiding from the media. No way she was going to let Lester Holt into her little world. She didn't want to be famous. If a story aired, probably her dad would see the thing somewhere in the corners of the world. She'd never be able to keep this whole thing secret. And her father was no angel, despite his name. He'd kill Anderson. Oh, yes, he would. Maybe he'd be sneaky about it by hiring a voodoo medicine woman to stick pins in an Anderson doll, or he'd invite Anderson to go skydiving and mess with his parachute, but boyfriend-icide was going to happen. Libby wasn't worried about it yet, because her dad didn't yet know for sure, but if she dropped the bomb, he'd drop a grenade on Anderson Kraft. Her dad had had enough of his daughter being hurt by bad guys.

Fuck, fuck, fuck. She hated Anderson. No, she hated what Anderson had done. But she loved Anderson. And if she tried to tell her father, or her professor, or even her goldfish that, she was done.

Right. As of right now, Libby didn't want anyone to know that she knew about what Anderson had done. Anyone. Even Anderson. Because if she didn't tell Anderson that she was a veritable cyber Nancy Drew, they could stay together. Sure, she'd always know that he had cheated off of her exam, but that wasn't so different from adultery, right? Couples got through cheating issues all the time. Here, her boyfriend had only touched her computer, delved into her written word, and used it for his own benefit. He hadn't touched breasts. He hadn't delved into . . . OK, this was heading back toward the topic of her father's tampon lesson email . . . any bodily part. And he hadn't given Libby — or Libby's computer — any diseases, viral or otherwise.

And she'd never be able to block out the fact that he'd created his mother's death out of whole cloth, stealing someone's else's real tragedy to get on Libby's good side. But maybe he'd really liked Libby? And she'd been refusing to let him in? And this was his way of showing how much he cared about her?

Libby knew that she couldn't ask for anyone's advice. Because she couldn't imagine that anyone would understand, and she was pretty sure that they'd tell her she had to turn Anderson in. That he was using her. Even that letting her potentially take the fall was tantamount to an abusive relationship.

The problem was, Libby had never felt completely fulfilled when she stood on her principles. So insisting on honesty and trustworthiness and all of that — it would make her honorable and pure, but it would also make her miserable.

There was only one answer. Libby needed to stay home, skip

classes, do whatever it took to avoid Anderson, Professor Shun, and all the future lawyers who surrounded her until she knew what she was going to do.

For all Libby knew, Anderson had his reasons. Maybe he was going through something. Maybe — oh, this could be it — maybe he was so overcome by his passion for Libby that he just couldn't think, just couldn't get himself to study, just couldn't find a way through the barricade Libby had been putting up. She'd been refusing him at that point. Boys got frustrated, right?

And now, if Libby turned him in, she'd have done him wrong three times. Once when she kept putting off his advances, thinking he wasn't the kind of guy who deserved her. Once when she doubted him after the meeting with Professor Shun, refusing to give him the benefit of the doubt. And now, when she went to Professor Shun and Dean Cerny and told them what had happened.

Libby switched back over to her Dahlia screen. And then she slammed the lid of the laptop. Even Dahlia Lithwick couldn't save her now. No, this one was all on Libby.

Eighteen

In ILT, Connie was leading the class in a discussion about a segment from "This American Life," NPR's beyond-fabulous show about real life situations that made people think. Today, she wanted the students to think some more about law and justice.

In this episode, the epic hottie Ira Glass was telling the story of a man who'd committed an armed robbery. Prison officials had made a clerical error and released him from jail before he'd served his sentence. Thirteen years later, after he'd become a father and a productive member of society, they tracked him down to take him back to jail. Was that justice? After all, the prison officials had messed up, inadvertently broken the rules. Should they be able to act as if nothing had ever happened, as if they'd never screwed up?

Connie looked to Libby to ask her opinion. She looked again. Libby wasn't in her seat in the front row. She called out in case Libby was backbenching it. "Ms. Behl?"

No answer.

"Has anyone seen Ms. Behl today? Or since Wednesday?"

The class murmured, shaking their heads. No one responded.

Then Mr. Sanders raised his hand. "I haven't, Professor, but maybe you should give her a ring."

The class fell apart in laughter. But Connie didn't laugh. It wasn't like Libby to miss class. Was she OK? It was one thing for a regular student — Ms. Jackson, maybe, or Ms. Patel — to ditch a time or two. But Libby seemed to thrive in the classroom. Honestly, Connie felt as if Libby brought the room to life. Anderson was there, of course, sitting in the back row, wearing his Harvard sweatshirt and looking as smug as Connie thought he always did.

Connie made a note on her legal pad to email Libby after class. And then she continued with the discussion of the best radio show, hosted by the hunkiest radio guy, *ever*.

•   •   •

When Professor Shun called on Libby and Libby didn't answer, Anderson Kraft sat up straight in his seat. Usually, in ILT, the best use of his time was catching up on sports news or reading the crappy but oh-so-juicy law school basher blog, Above the Law. Face it. Every ILT class was the same. They talked about law blah blah blah and justice blah blah blah and absolutely nothing that would ever help Anderson do a deal or draw up a contract when he was a lawyer someday.

But Libby loved ILT. She grooved on it. When they left class most days, the glow on her face was one Anderson had only seen her have in one other place. Of course, in that other place, the rest of her body tended to glow, too.

If Libby wasn't in ILT, that meant that there was something fishy going on. And, by fishy, Anderson didn't mean Breyer.

Anderson told himself to calm down, to breathe, not to jump to conclusions. Libby was probably just feeling under the weather. Or she'd gotten wrapped up in reading the transcript from a case that had been argued at the Supreme Court that morning. Or one of those social justice groups she belonged to needed a presence at a protest, stat.

The only weird part was that she hadn't texted him.

Maybe he was crazy, but, based on past experience, Anderson was worried that whatever was going on, he wasn't going to like it.

•   •   •

More than a week had gone by, and Libby was realizing that she only had one choice that would make her feel good.

Feminism be damned.

Whenever she thought about turning Anderson in or telling him she knew the truth about his mom, she felt like crap. Whenever she thought about holding Anderson in her arms, she felt amazing. That was so new for Libby — and unexpected — that she just couldn't let it go.

Maybe it was sleep deprivation (she'd been unable to do much more than toss and turn for days), maybe it was some kind of pathological form of co-dependency (yes, she'd Googled "love addiction" three or four times in the last several days). But however she'd gotten there, Libby had made a decision. She was going to copy the evidence about the exam and the stories about Jennifer Moreno onto a flash drive and hide it in the suitcase she never used any more. Not that she'd ever need the flash drive. That was the part she had to keep telling herself.

She was going to delete the tracking software on her laptop and clear the download history. And then she was going to go to Anderson and tell him that the sacrifice, her very-first-time-ever choice to allow the ends to justify the means, was worth it. Because they were worth it.

Oh, Christ. She sounded like a L'Oreal commercial.

Speaking of which, she probably ought to wash her hair. Or even just take a shower. Libby sniffed under her arms. Oh, yeah. She was starting to smell. A week in the same nasty "Real Men Don't Hit" T-shirt.

Libby took off her pajama pants and tossed them in the direction of the hamper, then turned the shower on full steam. Breyer wiggled his tail fin and blinked his eyes. Libby thought he approved.

In the shower, Libby sang along to her iPod, mounted to the tile wall in some waterproof contraption that Libby couldn't figure out but thanked the heavens for every day. She hummed through the part of the song that she didn't know. But then she belted it out. Taylor Swift seriously had it going on, especially when she sang about swallowing her pride. Libby had fallen in love with Anderson in the fall, but then the dark days had arrived. Tay-Tay seemed to have lived through the same damn thing.

●   ●   ●

Breyer swam near the surface of his bowl, seemingly sniffing the air. Libby laughed. God, it felt good to laugh. She was clean, she was resolved, and she was going to get her man back. No goldfish, no matter how loyal, was going to stop her. "I know, boy, smoked salmon pastries are an affront to your species, but they're Anderson's favorite. Not that I like them. No, I'd rather see my fish swimming around in a bowl than tender and moist in some egg custard and phyllo."

Breyer harrumphed. Or at least Libby thought he did. She made a note to Google later whether fishy disdain was even possible.

For now, she needed to get over to Anderson's with these mini quiches. If she hurried, she could use the key he kept under his mat and leave the snacks on his counter before Anderson got back from the afternoon Criminal Law lecture. She knew he'd stick it out until the end — the prof in that class was a riot, what with his toothy smiles and big Afro and affinity for hip hop music. And when Anderson arrived home, singing "Public Enemy," he'd burst out laughing at the sight of the plate full of tiny pastries. Ever since Libby had dumped them all over the snowdrift on the way to Professor Shun's Thanksgiving feast, and especially since Anderson had proposed picking them up and serving them anyway, they'd gotten a kick out of quiche.

OK, Libby would admit it. Law school turned regular, ordinary people into geeks. Geeks who got their laughs from tiny, cheesy pies. And even cheesier jokes.

At least they laughed about something. Quinn, on the other hand . . . Quinn kind of scared Libby. She took the whole "taking law school seriously" thing to the next level. Or maybe even the level after that.

Libby used a mini spatula to take the quiches out of the pan, stopping to suck on her index finger when she burned it on the hot metal. Someday, maybe she'd learn that rushing actually took longer in the end. Why hadn't she just let them cool? Why did she always make things so complicated?

But now she was ready. She loaded up a Tupperware container with her cheesy treats, separating each layer with waxed paper, feeling very Martha Stewart in the process. She grabbed her jacket, put on her hat, and clutched the plastic container close.

In fifteen minutes, she would be at Anderson's with her peace offering.

An hour or so after that, he'd call her.

And maybe two hours from now, they'd be cuddled on Libby's couch, all thoughts of cheating and lying behind them.

The way to a man's heart was through his stomach.

Libby talked herself through it. They were going to work things out. They were. Because — mamma mia! — she truly did not think that she could ever let Anderson go. Arriving at his garage apartment, her heart beat fast with excitement.

Libby balanced the container on the door handle as she bent down, felt under the mat, and located the key. The last thing she needed was another "it's raining quiche" episode.

She put the key in the lock, turned the handle, and felt the door give way. Eureka. She was in. Leaving the key in the door, she started down the hallway to the kitchen.

This was going to be great.

And then Libby stopped short in her tracks. Because coming from the end of the hall was a weird sound. It sounded like . . . screaming? Begging?

Libby shuddered. Someone was in Anderson's apartment.

Libby's heart pounded hard, but she remembered what her mom had always told her about how to handle anyone who wanted to hurt you — essential information for any New York kid. Scream as loud as you can. Know where the exits are. Grab anything you can use for a weapon. And go for the balls.

OK. Exit — front door. Check. Weapon — umbrella by the front door. Check. Balls. Libby hoped against hope that screaming would get the job done, even if it wasn't working for whoever was in the bedroom. Kicking someone — and, let's face it, the "someone" had to be Anderson — in the balls felt like more than she could handle, after all of the crappy events of the past few weeks.

She was still scared. She was still pretty sure she didn't have the physical oomph. But she knew that the law was a pretty mighty weapon. She'd gone to law school to make sure she knew the best ways to use that weapon to protect women like herself, and her mom, who had just gone out one beautiful day to help a bunch of people who needed it and ended up having it cost way too much.

Libby gathered all of her strength. "Hey," she called out. "Who's there? Get out right now. I've got a weapon, and I'm not afraid to use it."

Then she looked down at the umbrella in her hand. Come to think of it, maybe she would have to go with kicking the bad guy in the balls. This umbrella was one of the compact kind that folded into a little sleeve. It didn't even have a spike on the end. Libby could maybe whack someone over the head with it, but poking an eye out? Not going to happen.

The screams continued. "Anderson, I'm calling the police. I've got my phone out. They'll be here any minute, so you'd better let her go and get out of here."

The noises stopped. OK. Libby was getting somewhere. Still, she looked down at her sneakers. Could she castrate someone — Anderson — with them? Or rupture something? Did balls rupture? Or explode? Or . . .

Libby's thoughts were interrupted by the sound of rustling. She braced herself. And then she charged.

Afterwards, Libby would ask herself why exactly she hadn't figured out exactly what was going on in that bedroom. She would also wonder whether she'd actually have been able to kick Anderson — or anyone — in the balls. Because what she saw in that bedroom was at least as shocking as exploding testicles.

Standing by the bed, wrapped in a sheet, was Anderson. Looking hot and bothered. And only in part because Libby had just walked into his bedroom holding an umbrella in her fist like a bat.

The other reason that Anderson was all sweaty was in the bed. Naked. And smug. And smiling. Not crying. And no longer screaming.

Libby wondered for how many six-minute blocks the two of them had been there.

Quinn met Libby's eyes for a long minute, then turned away and pulled on her dress. She stuffed her bra and underpants into the bag sitting next to the bed, stood, and walked to the bedroom door.

She paused next to Libby. Then she turned and blew Anderson a kiss. She smiled at Libby and spoke. "Libby, I guess you've never really had it hot and heavy, huh? So that it makes you scream? Too bad.

"See you at C & B later for study group, OK, guys?"

And then it was just Anderson and Libby.

Libby wondered again about whether kicking someone in the balls would make the appendages explode. Finding out was sounding more and more appealing. Especially because the set in front of her now seemed to be shriveling and shrinking in what looked like fear. Or at least anxiety.

Anderson pulled on a pair of boxers and cleared his throat. "Look, Libby, this isn't what it looks like. You know that what you and I have is special. This thing with Quinn — honestly, it's not a big deal. She came on to me in a big way. She told me that she'd give me the transcripts she'd been making of our classes. And I figured, OK, why not? I'll spend one afternoon rolling around with Quinn, then I'll get the notes, and then I'll help Libby out because she's missed all these classes. I did it for you, Libby. Really. You have to believe me."

Libby put down the container of quiches. She lowered the umbrella. She spoke slowly.

"Real men don't eat quiche, Anderson. That should have been my clue. If you were a real man, you'd be faithful. If you were a real man, you'd take your own notes. If you were a real man, you'd come up with your own exam answers.

"If you were a real man, you'd stand on your own two feet and tell your own story, not steal someone else's to play the sympathy card.

"You had me fooled, Anderson. You even had Breyer fooled. But to my dad, it was as clear as a bell. You were nothing but a grody Harvard Boy. And now, I'm going to do everything possible to make sure that everyone knows it.

"You know, before I found you and Quinn in here, I was wondering whether kicking someone in the balls would make them burst or something. But now I know the truth. You can't rupture someone's balls when he doesn't have any balls. I guess that's sort of lucky for you — I couldn't destroy what you don't have.

"But I'll tell you something about me, Anderson. I finally realized something. And that is that it's time I grew a set."

Nineteen

Connie was sitting in her office, contemplating whether she should drive up to Bristol for a chocolate cabinet (or what she'd always called a "frappe" before she'd moved to Rhode Island) at the Daily Scoop. Her mouth watered. Why not take a drive? It was one of those gorgeous early March days when all the white and yellow daffodils were starting to bloom and people were starting to get their boats out of storage and onto the moorings. Heading up the island and across the bridge to what might be the cutest town in America sounded like just the thing to lift her out of the winter doldrums that always hit around now.

OK. She'd do it. Hell, yeah. One teeny weeny cabinet was not going to keep her from fitting into her pink dress. From the back of her office chair, she grabbed her leather car coat — a gift from James, who was always trying to spruce her up — and searched around on her desk for her keys. They weren't right next to her keyboard, where she usually dropped them when she came in, right before she rushed to the restroom. They weren't on the bookshelf next to her travel mug. They hadn't dropped into the trash can, had they? That had only happened once, years ago, but she'd been traumatized by the experience of rustling through her old candy wrappers and Diet Coke cans. No one should have to confront her vices that up close.

Connie was on her hands and knees, pawing through the grossness of her garbage — of course, today would be the day she'd decided to eat a mushy banana on her way to work but had dropped half of it into the trash, uneaten — when she heard a knock on her open office door.

"Professor Shun?" A voice rang out. "Are you in here?"

Crap. Should she answer? What the hell. This year alone, her students had seen her slip in coffee and land on her ass in front of the whole class, plus watched her cry over that PowerPoint that wouldn't show up on the screen no matter how many buttons she'd pushed. Ugh. Pomeranians. Well, she'd had the flu for that last one. That was a tiny bit of an excuse.

"Yes, hold on a minute!" Connie called. She struggled to her feet. Still no keys. Hair kind of messed up from hitting the office chair on the way down. At least her dress was around her knees instead of around her waist.

Connie stood and looked toward the door.

It was Libby. She was clutching a container full of quiches and crying. Her loose T-shirt read (had she put it on because she was so distraught?), " 'When we are born, we cry that we are come to this great stage of fools.' — William Shakespeare, *King Lear*. "

Uh, oh. An alarm bell went off in Connie's head. It sounded like maybe Libby had found out that someone was a fool. And Connie had a pretty good idea of who that might be.

•   •   •

Anderson was pacing in his apartment over Nana's garage. He needed to figure out how to breathe. When panic overtook him like this, he couldn't sit still. Usually, he'd go throw some rocks into the harbor or work on his rock wall or run along the beach, but for right now, he needed to stay right here. Libby would come back. She would. She loved him. She'd stomp off for a while, then she'd figure out that he'd been right, that his thing with Quinn had been meaningless (even if it had been going on a lot longer than the afternoon he'd claimed), and that he and Libby belonged together.

Even though he'd started the whole thing with Libby because he knew she was smart, he'd actually kind of liked her.

That was the reason that he hadn't called her over break. He had been feeling so guilty about the whole ILT exam thing, he hadn't known whether he could face her.

He hadn't felt guilty about the Quinn thing, not really. Quinn really did mean nothing to him. And he'd never figured that Libby would find out. The way Anderson saw it, Quinn was unlikely to be in law school much longer, not with her grades. Even if she didn't know how to use her transcripts of class discussions, though, Anderson did. And he'd thought they would help Libby out.

If you thought about it, Anderson was really doing Libby a favor. And that was what he'd tried to explain when she'd walked in — ugh — on him and Quinn. When the only reason he was even there with Quinn today was because Libby had been refusing to have anything to do with him.

Quinn would never have cut class, and so under normal circumstances, he wouldn't have been home, and Libby never would have found out, even if she had been talking to him. But Libby hadn't been going to class for a week or so, and so she'd missed the announcement that Crim was cancelled for today. And Quinn had beckoned. And he just hadn't thought there would be an issue.

At least Quinn had caught on that Anderson needed some space and had cleared out before Libby.

This wasn't like that other thing. With that girl. In college. Who had claimed that he had . . . No. Plus, neither Libby nor Quinn could make a claim that what he did with them was anything other than consensual. With Libby, once or twice, he'd even secretly set his iPhone to video during, just to make sure he could prove that she wanted it just as much as he did.

OK. Anderson was breathing better now. But where the hell was Libby?

•   •   •

Libby didn't know how to explain to Professor Shun what had happened. So much of it was totally unrelated to law school. The professor seemed like she really worked hard at not getting too personal with students — would she mind if Libby told her the truth, the whole truth, and nothing but the truth? Or would that be inappropriate?

And how did the fact that it seemed like maybe Professor Shun and her dad had made a love connection over Thanksgiving play in?

Well, she should probably just start with an offering. She held out the Tupperware container across the desk.

"Would you like a quiche? They're probably kind of cold by now, but they should be tasty. They're Anderson's favorite . . ." Libby started to cry again.

Professor Shun looked alarmed. "Sit down, Libby," the professor said.

Libby started to back out of the office. "No, it's OK, I'll just—"

"Libby, sit. What's going on? And, no, thanks, I think I'll pass on the quiche." The professor offered Libby a smile.

Libby sniffed. "It's just so embarrassing, it's hard to even start," she said.

"Just start at the very beginning," the professor answered. "And yes, I realize I just sounded like Julie Andrews, and no, I didn't mean to. You don't have to tell me about your favorite things, OK?"

Libby cracked a tiny grin. "How do you solve a problem like a liar?" she asked.

"A liar, huh? Called . . . ?"

"Anderson Kraft," Libby blurted.

"Ah." The professor sat back in her seat and folded her hands. "What has our friend the Harvard Boy been up to?"

Short of breaking out in song about how Anderson was a darling, or a demon, or a lamb, Libby wasn't sure how to start.

Professor Shun started off. "Libby, does this have anything to do with your ILT exam?" Libby sighed in relief. Professor Shun was asking the questions, and all Libby had to do was answer. She could do that.

"Professor Shun, I swear I don't know how this happened. I think it had to have been when the pizza man came. And I went downstairs to pay. Anderson likes pepperoni, and I like vegetarian, so I had to get two pizzas, and it took me a while to dig out my cash and then get back upstairs, and—"

Professor Shun held up a hand. "Libby, slow down. What exactly happened?"

Libby took a deep breath. Her professor was right. Keep it simple. "I am pretty sure that Anderson copied my ILT take-home from my laptop. When I was downstairs in my apartment building getting pizza."

The professor nodded. "Well, I can definitely see why you were crying, then. Did you know this at the time? Or did you just find out?"

Libby was a little stumped. How should she answer that? The honor code said she had to report misconduct, right? Did that mean that she had to do it immediately? Was she allowed to address it with the cheater first?

Professor Shun seemed to read her mind. "Libby, if you didn't do anything wrong, you're not in any trouble. The important thing is that we clear this up now."

Libby nodded. She cleared her throat and began. "I found out a couple of weeks ago. But I was trying to figure out what to do. Anderson . . . well . . . Anderson and I have been . . . and . . . so I didn't know if maybe I was overreacting, because I felt sort of betrayed, because I was so, well, into him, and the exams weren't even exactly alike anyway, so I thought that the 'beyond the reasonable doubt' standard wasn't satisfied . . ."

Professor Shun let Libby pause for a bit. And then she said softly, "But it sounds like you decided that you weren't overreacting?"

Libby took a deep breath. "Right. Because he did copy. I found a record of it on my computer cache. From the night when we . . . well, when we first . . ."

The professor broke in. "Libby, your personal life isn't my business. If you want to tell me about it, that's fine. But honestly, it sounds like it's really hard to talk about it."

Libby nodded slowly. "Yes, especially after I found him and Quinn in bed at his apartment today. And I also finally woke up and looked online and realized that he'd made up a whole story he'd told me about his mom being a nurse who was killed in Afghanistan." She stopped, unable to believe that she'd actually said that out loud. It made it real. Way too real.

Professor Shun looked stunned. "So he's a cheater in pretty much every way, is what you're telling me."

"Yes. He's a cheater in pretty much every way. He even said he was only sleeping with Quinn to get her class notes. He said he could relate to my mom's sacrifice because his mom had made a similar one. How can a guy like that ever represent clients? I don't even think that Anderson knows what the truth is, much less how to further it in the name of justice. He can't even follow rules."

Libby's professor seemed to understand exactly where she was coming from. "You know, Libby, every year, I see a student or two who really doesn't belong in law school. Maybe it's because he or she isn't cut out for it, just like I would be a total failure if I tried to go to art school—"

"That sort of sounds like Quinn. She really wants to be a lawyer. But she just doesn't seem to get it."

The professor nodded in agreement. "And then there are those who are way too cutthroat, way too interested in advancing them-selves, even at the expense of others. They usually think the rules don't apply to them, that anything is OK if it will get them an A. And they don't get that the very essence of being a lawyer — or a law stu-dent — is being ethical. That's why I focus so much on law and justice. Because they are the heart of what we do."

Libby took in her professor's words. "Yep. You pretty much just described Anderson to a 'T.' "

Professor Shun looked a little sad. "You know, Libby, I really hate it that you had to learn this lesson this way. He got you to like him. Maybe he even sincerely really liked you. But in the end, he liked him-self more. And that's the kind of guy you have to stay away from, no matter how appealing he might seem. A good friend of mine taught me that. And your dad has been hoping you wouldn't ever have to know that. He even emailed me, way back around Christmas, to ask me if I thought Anderson was OK. And, honestly, I couldn't say yes. But it's sort of unjust that when everyone else can see someone for who he is, the person it matters most to is blind."

Libby hated this. She hated everything about it. She felt about three feet tall. "Lady Justice is blind, but she still sees the truth," she answered.

"Yeah, Libby, but Lady Justice is a metaphor. Just like all of the other Roman gods. You can't hold yourself to the standard of some-one who isn't even real."

Libby felt herself withdrawing, no matter how kind and under-standing her professor was being. She needed some space. Some time to reflect. Maybe a good long conversation with Breyer. She stood. "Thanks, Professor Shun. What happens now?"

"What happens now is that I take this information you've given me and I hand it over to Dean Cerny. And then he'll decide what to do with it. I'm pretty sure he'll call Anderson in. And then Anderson will probably go before the Honor Board."

"And what about ILT?" Libby asked.

"You'll stay in ILT. Anderson may or may not. It's up to Dean Cerny."

"And there won't be any problem? With my ILT grade? Going forward?" More than anything, Libby didn't want this to reflect badly on her. She'd been dumb, it was true. Almost criminally dumb. The personal part of her life was kind of in shambles. The only thing that would help her get through it would be if the law school part of her life was unblemished.

"Libby, you're one of the best students I've had in a long time. Your only fault here was in trusting someone who turned out not to be trustworthy. I know this sucks. It really does. But maybe you can find it liberating, too? Moving on from it? Miss Liberty Behl?"

Libby laughed. "Yeah, when your name is Liberty, you kind of have to embrace it. So I will. Thanks, Professor Shun."

"No problem, Libby. Now go get yourself a cabinet or something. That's what we call a milkshake in Rhode Island."

"OK. Maybe not a cabinet. But maybe a really, really big banana split." Libby waved as she walked out of her professor's office.

•   •   •

"You go, girl," said Connie, when Libby was out of sight. Man, that had been a tough conversation. What a shitty situation for the kid to find herself in. But what a gutsy move she'd made, standing up for herself and showing Anderson Kraft that he couldn't mess with her. At least not anymore.

Connie gave up on her thought of a cabinet, at least for now. As yummy and satisfying as a chocolate milkshake sounded — especially when Felix was nowhere nearby to scarf half of it — she needed to email Bob Cerny.

From: Connie T. Shun <cshun@warrenlawschool.edu>
To: Bob Cerny <bcerny@warrenlawschool.edu>
Date: March 2, 2015 2:34:49
Re: Your day is about to get more exciting—NOT

Hello, Bob Cerny (you know there's just something about your name that calls for me to use both the first and last — such a ring to it),

Look out your window. Note the blooming crocuses. The shining sun. The water glistening only a few blocks away.

Now close your blinds. Because you and I ain't getting a single minute to bask in the glory of this spring day.

Students. They manage to ruin it every time.

Can we set up a meeting? I've just had a visit from a very upset student — the one we talked about a couple of months ago — who brought me some pretty damning evidence that her "boyfriend" (note the quotation marks) stole her ILT take-home, plus sold her a bunch of other bullshit. Besides the fact that she is devastated, she's loaded for bear. Could that have something to do with the fact that she caught him in the act of, shall we say, massaging class notes out of another classmate? Apparently, clothes were getting in the way of learning in that little rendezvous, so they'd taken them all off.

As you might imagine, this student has had an oh-so-lovely day, but I calmed her down and dispatched her to down a banana split. Now, lucky us, we get to deal with this. I'll head up to your office later with the documentation she gave me?

The stuff no one ever tells you about the joys of being a law professor . . .

Connie

Connie pressed "send," stood up and stretched. If she was going to be stuck at the law school all day, she probably ought to go home and walk His Royal Majesty Felix Frankfurter. He was going to be pissed. He'd been planning on spending the day digging up the neighbor's tulip bulbs, mere days before they'd been scheduled to burst into bloom. Now? He was going to be stuck inside, with only the Puppy Bowl Connie had recorded off Animal Planet to keep him occupied.

Connie was afraid. She was very afraid. Maybe she should stop at the hardware store on the way home and buy a padlock for her refrigerator door.

Onward.

·   ·   ·

Libby sat at her tiny dinette table, a pint of Ben & Jerry's Phish Food in front of her. She and Breyer enjoyed snacking together. They had an agreement that, when she sucked on the little dark chocolate fish in the ice cream, he politely turned his head away.

For right now, the goldfish was doing flips and spins in his bowl. Libby had told him that Anderson wouldn't be coming back, but that she was giving him a bloodworm lollapalooza to make up for it.

Suddenly, Breyer didn't seem to give a fig about Anderson.

And, more gradually, as more and more tiny chocolate fish swam down her throat, Libby found that she didn't, either.

Justice had been done.

Twenty

Connie and Bob Cerny sat at the small conference table in the dean's office, waiting for an appointment that would be, in technical dean speak, a wicked bummer. Their mood was glum, reflecting the weather outside. March was like that; one day was brilliant enough to inspire road trips for cabinets, the next was gloomy and misty. Connie picked at a loose thread on her skirt, one that had probably been there when she'd put the skirt away for the season back in September. Bob Cerny stroked the mustache that he'd waxed into a handlebar and fiddled with the manila folder in front of him. Except for the sound of incoming emails pinging in the dean's inbox, the room was silent.

Connie jumped at the knock on the door. Bob Cerny made an "it's groovy, stay calm" motion with his hands. He tilted his head at her and gave her a questioning thumbs-up. Connie took a deep breath and nodded. Here went nothing.

Bob Cerny stood, crossed to the door, and opened it. A twenty-something man in a grungy Harvard T-shirt waited on the other side. The guy's eyes were bloodshot and wary.

"Come in, Anderson," the dean said.

Kraft walked in, spotted Connie, and turned around. "I didn't know she was going to be here," he said, an accusing tone in his voice.

Bob Cerny spoke slowly. "Yes, Anderson, Professor Shun is here because the situation we're here to discuss took place in her class."

Kraft's face looked like he wanted to kill someone or flee. Fight or flight. Connie got the sense that even Kraft didn't know which one he'd pick, given his druthers.

Bob Cerny spoke first. "Anderson, do you know why Professor Shun and I have called you in today?"

"Dean, I've been through this with Professor Shun and with Libby. I didn't copy. If anyone copied, it was Libby, not me. We studied together! Of course our exams were going to be alike! And why has this gone on so long, anyway? It has been, like, two months." Kraft's voice rose so high he sounded like he might hyperventilate.

Connie picked some more at the thread on her dress. This was getting seriously uncomfortable. Why didn't Kraft get that they had the goods on him?

Bob Cerny waited for a minute, to let Kraft catch his breath, Connie thought. "Anderson, pretty much every student at this school is in a study group. In fact, from what Professor Shun has told me, in her class, you are required to be in a group. But we almost never have two exams or papers or whatever that look really similar. And that's because every student has his own individual voice and writing style. Each student has an original way at looking at a test question. Professor Shun is an experienced professor — she knows when two exams are just too similar to be coincidence. As for why it has taken so long, though, we've really wanted to be sure. So we did a thorough investigation before calling you in, over a period of more than a week."

Kraft's eyes flashed. His hands worked the knit fabric of his sweater. "Well, in this case, Professor Shun's experience was just wrong. And so was your investigation. I've got experience with this stuff. I know that administrators never get it right."

Bob Cerny sighed. He motioned to Connie. She bent down to her briefcase on the floor, pulled out a stack of papers, and handed them to the dean.

Bob Cerny extended the papers across the table to Kraft. "I'm sorry, Anderson, but it looks like the investigation was actually right on the money."

Connie and the dean watched as Kraft read the top sheet. He looked up.

"Where did you get this?"

Bob Cerny met Kraft's eyes. Connie's were still focused on the tabletop. "Where we got it doesn't matter. What does matter is that Libby Behl's computer cache history shows that her take-home exam was downloaded to a USB drive. A USB drive that had never been used on this laptop before, the forensic computer people found. And, Anderson, we're pretty sure that that USB drive belonged to you. Its name was 'Kraft.' "

Kraft broke out in a sweat. His breaths came fast. To Connie, it looked like he wanted to jump out of his chair and run. He'd chosen. Flight. Except that he couldn't really do that in the Dean's office.

Connie waited. Bob Cerny followed her lead.

The silence dragged on as Kraft fought to breathe. Bob Cerny finally spoke up. "Anderson, could I get you a drink of water?"

Kraft rubbed his temples, then spoke. "No, thank you, Dean. Look, so I guess you know I downloaded Libby's exam. But it's not fair to put this on me. It wasn't my fault."

Bob Cerny leaned toward Kraft and nodded. "Tell me about that, Anderson. How was it not your fault?"

Kraft's words came out in a rush. "Well, I mean, first Professor Shun put us all in a study group together. And Quinn Everly — I mean, come on. Quinn is not the sharpest knife in the rack. She's more like a spoon or something. So that left Libby and me to do all the work. And it was so clear in class that Professor Shun thought Libby hung the moon or something and hated me—"

Connie spoke up. "Now, wait a minute—"

Bob Cerny kept his eyes locked on Kraft and held his hand up to Connie to let the student speak.

"And then there was that whole thing with the dress—"

Bob Cerny turned a confused face to Connie. Connie's face reflected his own confusion back at him. As far as she knew, Monica Lewinsky had been nowhere near the law school, but the way this semester was going, who knew? Bob Cerny spoke again. "The dress?"

Kraft's voice was even, but his eyes glimmered. "Yeah, Professor Shun's dress. To be honest, Dean Cerny, I've been wanting to tell you about it for a few months now, but I didn't want to cause trouble, and plus Professor Shun was grading me, and I figured she might, like retaliate or something. Like I said, it's pretty clear she hates me. Has since August."

Bob Cerny looked at Connie again. She gave him a "got nothing" look. The dean turned back to Kraft.

"Anderson, neither Professor Shun nor I has any idea what you're talking about. But it doesn't sound like it has anything to do with your copying Libby Behl's exam."

"It does, though. After Professor Shun harassed me on the beach, I figured I needed to do well in her class. And I didn't feel comfortable going to her office after that, like to ask her questions or anything. Who knows what she would have done?"

A look of comprehension mixed with horror crossed Connie's face. Oh, crap. The dress. And the zipper. And Felix. Needing to crap. And the beach. And Kraft. Way back to just after Thanksgiving. When she was just getting over the flu.

Kraft caught the look on her face and narrowed his eyes. She knew exactly what he was talking about. He knew she knew. He pressed his advantage. "So I had to copy. And it wouldn't be fair to punish me when it wasn't my fault."

Bob Cerny cleared his throat. "Anderson, the rules say you can't copy. It's in the Student Handbook. We talked about it at Orientation. You signed a pledge saying you understood. I have a copy of it right here in your file." The dean held up the manila folder on the table.

"And accusing Professor Shun of something — I don't even know what — is not an excuse for breaking those rules. If you thought Professor Shun did something wrong, the right way to handle it would have been to come see me and let me deal with it."

Kraft's voice grew high again. "I couldn't do that. You were biased, too. You're dating her best friend. You're always walking together down at my end of the beach. And not just walking."

Bob Cerny flushed. Connie slowly turned and looked at him. The dean did not meet her eye.

"Anderson," Bob Cerny continued. "There are a lot of things we don't know here. What you're talking about with the dress. Where you get the idea that I'm biased. Even why you would think that Professor Shun would retaliate against you. But we do know that you lied, lied consistently about copying from Libby, and even said that if copying happened, Libby did it. So you can complain all you want that it isn't fair, that the rules should be waived in this instance, but you'll get nowhere with me with that argument."

Kraft half stood. "But—"

Bob Cerny's voice grew stern. "No 'buts,' Anderson. Professor Shun has prepared an Honor Board complaint. You'll be served with a copy of it. I need to tell you that the penalty for cheating and lying is, at the very least, failing the course. Most of the time, though, students who are convicted are expelled. So I need you to be ready for that possibility. I'm really sorry that it came to this, Anderson. You're a bright guy. You could have done well here. If you'd like, I can recommend a counselor to help you through this tough time."

Kraft stood. "Yeah, somehow I don't think a counselor is going to do it. I'm going to look into getting a lawyer over this. Professor Shun—" Kraft pointed at Connie. "—sexually harassed me. She put me in a situation I couldn't handle. And then she called me out for cheating when she formed the study group. She should be forced to leave this law school, not me."

Bob Cerny lowered his voice even more. "Anderson, if you do stay in school, you'll take an Evidence class and learn a bit about credibility. And you'll figure out that you have none. So, if I were you, I'd stop there." Bob Cerny held his arm toward the door. "I'll walk you out. Professor Shun, could you wait here for me?"

Connie nodded. The loose thread on her dress was opening up into a hole. One Connie wished she could fall through.

Bob Cerny showed Kraft out. Connie jumped a little when she heard the outer door to the Deans' suite slam. And then the dean walked back in.

"OK, so," Bob Cerny said. "Looks like we've got a lot to talk about. The good news is that Anderson admitted to copying from Libby. We should be able to handle that drama pretty efficiently now.

"The bad news is that Anderson seems to think that he's got the goods on both of us, that he managed to call *us* on the carpet. He knew — and I'm thinking you didn't — that I am dating Sarah. And he thinks that you sexually harassed him? Actually, I'm pretty sure he doesn't think you did, but he thinks he can use some random interaction against you. So, you want to start, or you want me to?"

Connie didn't know whether to cry or scream. She liked Bob Cerny. Apparently her best friend really liked Bob Cerny. But Connie didn't know him all that well.

What the heck. "I'll start," said Connie. "Has Sarah told you about James?"

Bob Cerny nodded and stroked his mustache as Connie spilled the story. About the dress. And needing James to zip it. And cursing James for the millionth time for not being there. And Felix insisting on his walk. And encountering Anderson.

"And then I asked him to zip the dress. 'No problem,' he told me. He said he helps his Nana all the time. And I had on a camisole under it! The most he saw was my shoulders! But I wondered at the time whether I was breaking my own 'no getting personal with students' code. I've just been trying so hard to get past that."

Bob Cerny started to laugh. "And he saw Sarah and me kissing on the beach, and he figured that was his trump card. Got something on the prof. Got something on the dean. The thing is, neither of those things actually *is* anything."

Connie squinched her eyes at the dean. "Really?" She thought for a second. Huh. Bob Cerny was probably right.

And then Connie started to laugh, too. "The irony is that this is the guy who always argues in class that we should apply the rules consistently. We shouldn't deviate, even if we could achieve justice that way."

"Rules apply to everyone but him. Right. It's a type. Plus, I seriously think he's got some unresolved issues with women. Libby Behl? Quinn Everly? You? He's tried to manipulate all of you. Plus, he had an incident in undergrad that the admissions committee had to discuss before they admitted him. He'd been accused of bullying a woman online, stalking her, writing crazy things about her, posting photos where he'd put her face on someone else's naked body. She'd been so scared and freaked out that she'd dropped out of school. The administration had never been able to prove it was him — most of it was posted from public computer terminals in the library — but he had to include the charge in his law school application because he was subject to an inquiry, and we need to know about that stuff so we can consider whether students will have issues being admitted to the bar when they graduate." Bob Cerny looked more solemn.

Connie nodded. She felt like she'd always known something was off about Kraft. Angel sure had. She just had never known exactly what. But . . . "It's just that, I guess I sort of inherently trust people who went to Harvard. Sure, it was kind of a tough place in many ways. But Sarah and I met some of the best people we'd ever known there. There were so many people who were doing amazing things, fighting for justice—"

Bob Cerny interrupted. "Connie, I'm sorry, I'm not following. What does trusting people who went to Harvard have to do with anything?"

Connie gave him a confused look. "Well, I guess I tried to give Kraft the benefit of the doubt because he went to Harvard. Even when every cell in my body was screaming at me that he was scum."

Bob Cerny was silent for a beat. Then he opened the manila folder he'd placed on the conference table before their meeting with Kraft. He read for a moment, pressed his lips together, and looked up at Connie.

"Right, Connie, I get it. Except for one thing. Anderson didn't go to Harvard."

The two of them looked at each other for a quiet moment. And then Connie threw up her hands. "Well, that shows you what happens when you make assumptions. And, shit, this explains why he's got a really skewed idea of justice." Connie laughed so hard that tears started running down her cheeks.

Bob Cerny stroked his mustache. And then he looked down at the folder again. "I'm thinking that a University of Southern New York T-shirt isn't quite as awe-inspiring to the girls."

Connie wiped her eyes. Laughing so hard had spread her mascara down her face. "OK, so when are we going to talk about you and Sarah?"

·   ·   ·

Later that evening, Connie sat on the sofa, looking out at the water, rubbing Felix's belly. Every time she paused to take a sip of her wine or type something on her laptop, the little dog took his nose and nudged her hand. Going back and forth — keyboard, belly, keyboard, belly — it took her almost ten minutes to compose a four-line email to Sarah.

From: Connie T. Shun <cshun@warrenlawschool.edu>
To: Sarah Abernathy
          <judge_abernathy@rid.uscourts.gov>

Date: March 10, 2015 20:32:17
Re: Liberty and justice for all

So, Your Honor,

We got the guy.

And, um, you got the guy, too, or so I hear?

Sounds like we have some things to talk about.

Speaking of getting the guy, should I be shopping for a dress?
No ruffles. No yellow. Or I'll have Felix engage in a search and
destroy mission.

Connie (remember me?)

P.S. Bob Cerny? Really?

Connie read over her email. Too harsh? Nope, just the facts, ma'am. She pressed "send," pulled it up, read it one more time, reassured herself that it was fine, then closed her laptop.

"It's just you and me, boy," she said to Felix. "Don't you go running off with Madame Pomeranian, now."

Felix groaned in his sleep. Connie smiled. Yeah, no. Her little wiener dog would never leave her. Just watch him try.

Connie adjusted her knee just a bit, all the better to let Felix snuggle down. She placed her empty wine glass on the coffee table in front of her. And then she closed her eyes.

When she woke to the sound of the snowplow outside her house, it was dark. Felix was on his red bed, his copy of the Constitution under his nose. Her wine glass smelled sour. Her neck had a crick that she'd be lucky to banish by this time next week.

Connie stood, picked up her wine glass, and trudged into the kitchen. On the counter, her iPhone chirped at her. She'd forgotten to plug it in, and now it was fussing. "Battery low! Below 20% charge!" the screen read.

Connie picked it up, ready to take it into her bedroom and put it in the iHome on her nightstand, when an email lit up the screen.

From: Sarah Abernathy
          <judge_abernathy@rid.uscourts.gov>
To: Connie T. Shun <cshun@warrenlawschool.edu>
Date: March 10, 2015 20:45:18
Re:Re: Liberty and justice for all

Jeez, Louise,

OK, so it has been a weird time, and I've had to keep some stuff to myself.

Honestly, I didn't want to tell you about my dating life because I was afraid it might make you feel like I was leaving you, too. We had enough of that with James.

But seriously, isn't that Bob Cerny a total hottie?

It's a bit premature for shopping, but I will promise you no yellow. Can't commit yet on ruffles. You know I'm sort of a ruffle kind of girl. One reason I became a judge — I get to wear one around my neck whenever I want. Two, even. Who's gonna stop me?

Friend of mine, let's talk about what's really going on here. You're sassing a federal judge. Ha! You're ready to get more personal with people again. You're ready to have others share.

It has taken a while after James. But you're there.

I'll show you mine if you'll show the students yours? (She says in James's oh-so-fabulous voice.)

And now — off on a date with a hunky guy. You might know him? Name's Bob Cerny?

By the way, love the re: line here. They should put it in a song or a poem or a pledge or something.

Love. Always. Don't you forget it.

Sarah

P.S. You might not be a judge, but you're sure doing your part in making sure the future lawyers of the world think about justice. Remember how much James loved Tom Hanks in *Philadelphia*? We watched it on DVD back when we were in law school? And James told us that he finally got why we were in law school? "What I love the most about the law," Tom Hanks said in playing an associate at a big law firm, "is that every now and again — not that often, but occasionally — you get to be part of justice being done. It really is quite a thrill when that happens."

As your best friend, it really is a thrill to watch you being a part of justice being done.

Connie smiled a tiny little smile. She could just hear Sarah talking in James's oh-so-fabulous voice, so to speak. And if she could never hear the real thing again, she was glad Sarah brought it out for an airing every once in a while.

.   .   .

Anderson was standing on the beach, just down from Nana's house, looking around for the biggest rock he could find. He needed something that would make a major splash, a real dent when it landed in the ocean. Even though the dark made it harder to find stones to throw, at least it hid his frustration.

Anderson felt like nothing he said or did at Warren made a difference. He needed impact.

That professor. And that dean. They just didn't get it.

No one got it. Ever. Not his parents. Not the administration at U of SNY. Not even, it would now appear, Libby.

He'd never thought Quinn got it, and he hadn't expected her to. In this, of all things, he'd told Libby the truth. No, he hadn't gone to Harvard. Yes, he had copied her midterm. No, his mom hadn't been a nurse who died in Afghanistan — she was alive and well and Secretary of the Greenwich Junior League. But truly, no, Quinn had not meant a thing to him. All she'd been was a source — a source for notes. Once he'd seen that she'd really transcribed all of their classes and study sessions, he'd figured she was the key to acing law school. Yeah, no.

He'd lost Libby because, the truth? It was too hard for Anderson to handle.

And now it looked like he'd probably lose law school, too.

But here's what Anderson knew: If he could keep lifting the big rocks, if he could keep making a big splash, if he could hold his head high and pretend everything was OK, he could probably get through even this.

There was no way some little things like a clueless prof, a vengeful ex-girlfriend, and, yes, OK, some issues with anxiety were going to stop him.

•   •   •

Libby sat on her sofa, laptop booted up, floor lamp dimmed, reading the latest updates on SCOTUSblog. She hadn't felt this free in months, years, really — plus, mid-March was always a prime time for interesting cases to be argued. Three years ago, there had been Obamacare; two years ago, gay marriage; last year, the contraceptive mandate.

But, for once, reading about the Supreme Court was only a distraction. There was something else she really needed to read about.

Libby opened her browser, clicked on Google, and typed in "FDNY memorial 9/11." And then she started to look at the photos. There was Chaplain Mychal Judge, whom her mom had praised over and over again for being so good with victims of fires and accidents. There was paramedic Carlos Lillo, with whom her mom had often ridden out to some emergency. He had loved the outdoors, his obituary said, and he'd been so excited to get married in Jamaica. There was Ricardo Quinn, another paramedic who had responded, like her mother, even though he wasn't assigned to go to the Towers that day.

After several hours, Libby closed her eyes for just a minute and let herself drift. Now she'd used the rules to make sure that justice was done in this whole mess with ILT — she'd won this time! — she felt mostly OK about letting herself envision her big dream — prosecuting terrorists at the Hague, sending them off to prison forever, keeping them from ever hurting anyone again.

Or even — could she really go this far, be this sure of herself? — standing in front of the nine Justices, cranking the handle that made the podium go up and down, and arguing with passion about how the Court could do justice.

Breyer swam to the front of his tiny courthouse and seemed to pose. If ever there were fishy justice to be done, Breyer would be the guy to do it. The only thing was that Libby suspected he wanted to wear a powdered wig, and they didn't do that at the United States Supreme Court. The lawyers in the Solicitor General's office wore morning suits, but that was about as close to true dapper style as Breyer could ever possibly get. If Libby knew her fish, though, she would bet a bucket of bloodworms that he'd have a goldfish tailor all lined up.

Libby opened a new window and switched over to email. She had to tell her dad the good news. The only problem was that it would vindicate all his bad feelings toward Anderson. As much as Libby knew her dad was right, she hated to tell him that.

Oh, what the hell. Let the guy live a little.

From: Libby Behl <lbehl@warrenlawschool.edu>
To: Angel Behl <abehl@foodandtravelwriters.com>
Date: March 10, 2015 21:04:36
Re: Out of troubled waters

Daddy dearest,

I'm covering my ears, so you can say it: "I told you so."

The bad news is that Anderson is a totally grody Harvard Boy who could teach Scuzzy Dude a few new tricks.

The good news is that Dean Cerny and Professor Shun know it, and he won't be bothering me no more.

Breyer is kind of devastated. He really was digging having someone to guy talk with.

Me? Not so much. Somehow, I think that with Anderson out of the picture, the rest of this school year will be smooth sailing.

And the other good thing here was that I've really gotten to see Professor Shun (a.k.a., your crush) in action. Holy smokes, that woman rocks. Yes, that's a hint, Daddy. As in, don't let this one get away. There might be many fish in the sea, but they aren't Connie Shun.

Miss you, Daddy. But I'm doing OK. I really am. It feels like the scales of justice have truly tipped.

Libby

With her email soaring through cyberspace, Libby looked over at Breyer's bowl. The little dude was cruising slowly, barely moving his tail, the epitome of fishy relaxation. Libby blew him a kiss. The goldfish responded with a few bubbles. Libby lay back on the sofa, closed her eyes, and dreamed of morning suits.

•   •   •

Connie woke, blinking, to bright sunlight. Felix Frankfurter stretched out beside her, his head under her chin, his tail down around her waist, amazingly still asleep at . . . Connie checked the clock . . . 8:32 a.m. Connie checked to make sure the little dog was breathing. This never happened. But yes, the small red dog was snoring away, somehow having gotten the message that Connie had needed some serious z's.

She hoped this didn't mean that he'd been sticking his tongue in her wine glass again.

Connie scooped Felix up in her arms and cradled him like a baby. He blinked crossly, then licked her nose. She opened the sliding door to the deck, tossed him out, and told him, "Go chase a butterfly, Felix." Then she shut the door firmly, ignoring his scratching on the pane, and crossed the kitchen to start the coffee.

While it brewed, Connie opened her email. She scrolled. It looked like there was nothing from Bob Cerny . . . good. That meant that the report to the Honor Board had gone smoothly and he was on to other things. Nothing from Sarah . . . not surprising. Her best friend had had her say in her email last night. If Connie knew Sarah, the judge would sit tight now, waiting for a response, then propose an evening of mani/pedis, chocolate, and white wine. Preferably all at once.

Just as Connie was about to close down and open the door for Felix, her computer pinged. She scrolled back to the top of her email screen and looked.

She closed her eyes, shook her head, and rolled her shoulders.

And then she checked again to make sure that wine hadn't gone to her head in some weird way.

It hadn't.

What she'd thought she'd seen? It was still there.

She had her first email from Angel since December. Featuring a photo of him in a captain's uniform. He even had the number of stripes right, something Connie only knew because of the whole Captain-Crunch-isn't-a-captain debacle.

From: Angel Behl <abehl@foodandtravelwriters.com>
To: Connie T. Shun <cshun@warrenlawschool.edu>
Date: March 11, 2015 23:48:12
Re: Turbulence has subsided

Professor Connie,

I've been sailing around the Strait of Gilbraltar on a small ship, speaking Spanish, learning about masts and helms, and trying to keep the contents of my stomach from coming back up to see the light of day.

A few days ago, the sea was high, the ship was rocking, and the guys at the wheel seemed pretty intent. It's never a good sign when the crew isn't joking, isn't laughing, isn't even talking. It means they're working hard to steer the ship through rough waves.

The passengers? They just have to trust that the crew members know what they're doing. Eventually they'll get the ship to smooth water, the guests know, but the journey there is sometimes no fun at all. Most feel sick, and scared, and alone on the wide, deep sea. They might choose to sit by themselves, hugging their life vests close, looking for shore on the horizon.

Crossings can be hard, but landings are always fine.

When the landing comes, it's time to open back up again, the passengers know. To revel with their shipmates and drink champagne. To pat the crew on the back.

I know Libby's been through some rough seas of late. Something tells me that you have, too. But the shore is in sight. Pop open a bottle. Tell stories. Laugh.

And then you'll have your sea legs back.

Connie, my dear, you're one of the finest captains I have met in these travels of mine. Show the passengers what you're made of. They'll trust you all the more.

Riding the wave's a balancing act, it's true. But, boy, you don't want to miss the view from the top.

Your first mate (would that it were so),

Angel

Connie stared at the screen. Rough waters. Land in sight. Showing her passengers that she knew what she was doing.

Angel sometimes seemed more like a philosopher than a travel writer. Maybe the two weren't mutually exclusive.

But making it through the turbulent sea to land had loosened Connie up. She could feel herself relaxing, from her forehead to her shoulders to her belly to her toes.

Keeping it all inside, controlling the ship's path seemed logical, but it wasn't working for her. Maybe Angel was right. Maybe she needed to ride the waves and see what happened. Maybe she needed to look at all of this from a different point of view.

Maybe . . . OK, yes. Definitely. It was time to tell some stories.

Twenty-One

Connie stood at the front of the classroom. It was a warm April day. The windows were open. The class was quietly sleepy. Everyone was mellow except for Quinn, whose tap, tap, tap had become the rhythm and melody of ILT.

Connie began. "You know, I've been teaching for many years now, and I've always felt it was important to do as most lawyers do: keep my personal life separate from what I do here, in the classroom.

"My best friend, James, always used to tell me that I was wrong. He thought I could do real justice — make truly reflective, effective lawyers — by showing students my real self. He thought that students should know that juggling a personal life with a professional life was far from easy, but that great lawyers were whole people, people who cared about others.

"Right up until the day he died, James would tease me that I was a cardboard cut-out of a law professor. And so, today, I've decided to listen to him." Connie looked up at the ceiling. "James, baby, if you're tuning in, here goes nothing."

Connie clicked her clicker. An image of a dark-haired man, in his thirties, appeared on the screen. He was smiling at the person taking the photo.

"James Meisner was my best friend starting way back when we met freshman week in college. We were total opposites. He was this flamboyant, dishy sculptor who'd give you a big kiss on each cheek the first time he met you. I was a straight-laced rule follower with glasses. Naturally, I fell head over heels in love. That lasted about a year, until James came out to me and told me he was really into this guy on our hall."

Connie clicked the remote again. An older photo filled the screen. James was wearing a "Make Love, Not War" T-shirt. Connie was wearing a peasant top and had her hair braided over the top of her head. They were both wearing platform boots and dancing to something. From the looks of the photo, the "something" was probably ABBA. Why the heck they were doing the early '70s thing was probably best forgotten.

"I'd never met a gay person, or at least I didn't think I had. Back in the small town where I grew up, it probably wasn't safe to be gay. It sure wasn't very safe to be different."

Ms. Jackson nodded her head, slowly. She leaned back in her seat.

"You'd have thought that I'd have been put off by James. He was nothing like me. But he just exuded love, and caring, and fun. And he sort of forced me to be his friend. Really, he should have been put off by *me*. I was sort of rigid. And high strung. And anxious. But I've always counted it among the greatest things in my life that he was drawn to me, that he saw something in me that I didn't see. He thought I was smart, and insightful, especially when I wasn't self-conscious. That was news to me. But college was a time when James and I both did a lot of self-discovery. Whenever what I discovered was kind of hard to take — like that I hated Shakespeare's plays but loved the bad boys who were totally emotionally unavailable — I'd tell James about it, and we'd go out for donuts."

Connie clicked again. This time, she and James were pictured in their graduation gowns. She was smiling seriously for the camera. James was bonking her over the head with a rolled-up diploma.

"When I went off to law school, James came with. He said that Boston was one of the great art cities in the country. He'd sculpt in the loft we rented across the river from South Station and visit the museums on the weekends, he said. He'd cook for me, he said. He'd walk me home when I took the T back from Harvard Square, late at night, he said. Looking back, I think that James was probably just as afraid of the big, bad world after college as I was. But James was brave. James made his luck. James made great things happen.

"When I met Sarah Abernathy during my 1L year, James could have been jealous. Sarah was the first friend I'd bonded with anything like I had with James. And maybe he was jealous, who knows. But he chose to embrace her, just like he had embraced me. Sarah moved into the loft. We all stayed up late nights, Sarah and I studying, James sculpting or making up crazy kinds of lattes to keep us going. Our favorite was Butterbeer — a combination of cinnamon syrup, caramel, milk, and toffee sprinkles."

Connie clicked. James was holding a giant coffee carafe in one hand and a bottle of cinnamon syrup in the other. Connie and Sarah were both licking foam mustaches from their upper lips and crossing their eyes. Sarah had been holding the camera for the photo, Connie remembered, and James had insisted on her taking five or six so that his smile didn't look crooked. Sarah and Connie had been rolling their eyes over more than just the lattes.

"And then I got a teaching job here, at Warren. Sarah and James figured that living in the Ocean State sounded grand. We all moved down together. James lived with me here in Newport. Sarah got her own place in Providence, because she was working at a big firm there and billing lots of hours. Oh, and for about twenty minutes, she was actually married. Even during the marriage that you could have blinked and missed, on the weekends, Sarah would come down here and stay with James and me. We'd go to the beach, then head out for drinks."

Connie clicked. Three photos lined up across the screen. In one, Sarah was wearing a black robe. In the second, Connie was holding up a letter and giving a thumbs-up. In the third, James was raising a glass of champagne and standing in front of a sculpture of a giant pair of lips.

"Then Sarah got appointed to be a judge. I got tenure. James had his first gallery show. Life was so damn good.

"None of us was too great at love. I dated a series of — you guessed it — losers. Sarah tried every form of Internet dating there was and ended up with nothing but hysterical stories. James? James just thought everyone he met was fabulous.

"But that didn't mean that we didn't flirt with any damn person we liked. James, especially. And that's why I'm telling you this story.

"You see, one year ago this week, on a Saturday, Warren was holding an evening open house for prospective students. I agreed to attend, to teach a sample class.

"Sarah took the train up to Boston. She was the keynote speaker at an NAACP event.

"James was bored. His weekend pals were deserting him. And so he decided to go out. To a gay bar. On the boardwalk.

"And he never came home."

Connie clicked to a slide with three mug shots.

"That night, three thugs attacked him leaving that gay bar. They beat him up. Two of them held him down on the ground, and the third stabbed him through the chest. Three times. The police think the first wound killed him. He didn't suffer, they said. At night, when I can't sleep, I hold my dachshund in my arms and tell myself over and over that James didn't suffer. He went straight to heaven that night. No pain. No tears. No anger that Sarah and I weren't there.

"But Sarah and I were determined to lock his killers up for life. These thugs. These gaybashers. Let them see how they liked getting beat up. We hoped that would happen in prison. And sending them to prison? It should be a cinch.

"The police had the guys in custody. They had fingerprints on the knife. They had the thugs' clothes, covered in James's blood.

"The two things they didn't have? A legal search. And a properly elicited confession.

"You see, the police had been so angry by what they'd seen that night that they just said 'to hell with the rules of criminal procedure.' They followed an anonymous tip to the guys' house, and they just busted their way in. They found the knife and the clothes pretty quickly — the guys hadn't even had a chance to ditch the evidence. Then they grabbed the guys, forced handcuffs on them, and told them they'd better admit what they did or they'd make sure they never saw daylight.

"By this point in the year, you can probably guess what happened. Before they went to trial, their lawyers moved to suppress the knife, the clothes, and the confessions. The jury shouldn't hear about that evidence, they said, because the police acted illegally.

"The judge agreed. He refused to allow the evidence to be admitted. And without it, the DA just didn't have a case he could win. As far as I know, the guys who killed James are still walking around Newport, grabbing coffee down by the wharf, having a drink at their favorite bar, laughing about the night they got away with killing a disgusting fag.

"You know, we've reached the end of the year, but in a lot of ways, we've come back around to the beginning. We started out the year talking about law and justice. How do they intersect? How do they diverge?

"So, you tell me. Should law have prevailed — should James's murderers have gone free because the police did what they did? Or did the law prevent justice from being done? Because, you know, there's no doubt that these guys did it. Because Sarah and I still cry. James gave us both so much. And we can't even give him the satisfaction of knowing, from that cloud where he's eating bon bons and mixing up

Butterbeer lattes, that his murderers are in prison."

Sarah Abernathy stepped out the shadows. "We did our best, girl. And James, you'd better send us a sign that you know it."

The class was silent. They waited. No butterflies flew in through a window. No wind chimes tinkled. No lights suddenly turned themselves on or off.

Sarah crossed her arms and looked up. "Dammit, James, you never were the quiet type. I'm not sure why you have to start now."

Sarah walked over to her friend and put her arm around her shoulder. The judge faced the class. "You all know what? This professor here, she's brave, people. She told me earlier this week that she was going to try to open herself up and tell you about James. To be honest, I didn't think she'd do it. I came over to cheer her on just in case.

"Who's with me?"

In the front row, Libby Behl stood and clapped. And clapped harder. And stomped.

Then she climbed on her seat and clapped some more. She did not fall off.

Beside her, Quinn Everly closed her laptop. She stood. She roared.

One by one, Connie Shun's ILT students rose from their seats and cheered.

Ms. Jackson. Mr. Matthews. Mr. Lee. Ms. Patel. And even Bob Cerny, who'd gotten a call that a mighty ruckus was going on in Room 212.

He winked at Sarah. She winked back.

The only person who did not stand was Anderson Kraft. His seat was empty. He'd skipped this last ILT class. Odds were, under the honor code rules, he'd fail the class and have to take it again, anyway.

Connie waited for the hoopla to die down. "So, I'd like to leave you with one final thought. I'm hoping that, over the course of your 1L year, you've had issues in your own lives that made you think deeply about how you could use the law to do justice, or about how law has gotten in justice's way.

"But what I'm hoping you've found, over the course of this year, is that a good lawyer can help David beat Goliath. That lawyer — perhaps even one who came from an unprivileged background — can use the law as a powerful slingshot to fight her way to justice.

"Sarah and I did not succeed in doing that for James. But maybe — just maybe — one of you will be able to help someone you love.

"And if you do, I'll be there, cheering you on."

Epilogue

Only a few months later, on a bluebird day . . .

Liberty Behl: It seemed like it was impossible that it was actually May. The sun was shining. The ocean was turning blue. Even Breyer's scales seemed a brighter shade of orange. As for Libby? Since she'd tossed her coat and hat into the storage box under her bed, she'd shed an old skin — as well as her hatred of bluebird days and Anderson Kraft.

Maybe it had something to do with the fact that she'd ended up second in the class, with a GPA of 3.85. Who'd have thunk it? Maybe it was because, on the day she'd gotten her grades, she'd joined the "Warren Students for Justice" association. Maybe it was because Angel was coming to Newport for the summer, with plans to go back and forth to Block Island on a writer's retreat.

As for law school, by the end of the school year, it had come to fit Libby like a brand new skin. The best part about it? She liked this particular skin a lot.

Connie Shun: With the school year over and a sabbatical coming up, Connie was thinking about making some major changes. After a year of mourning James, she needed to get on with life — or at least, that was what he'd seemed to be telling her with that tiny earthquake that had shaken Newport last week. And don't even try to tell her that hadn't been James sending her a message. Newport didn't get earthquakes, or not ones you could feel, anyway.

Connie's plan? A summer of enjoying beautiful Rhode Island beaches, then several weeks of traveling, maybe even months. Lucky for her, Felix was small and flexible. He wouldn't like being under the seat in front of her. But maybe it was time for Connie to take charge there, too.

And if Connie and Felix happened to hang out with a certain elder Behl in Tanzania or Japan? Well, she'd decide about that if it happened. One thing she knew for sure: The guy knew how to ring her bell.

Anderson Kraft: Anderson wasn't so crazy about law school. For the first time in his life, he hadn't been able to make things go his way. His final GPA? Only a 2.79, placing him just below the middle of the class. It wasn't his fault he'd done so poorly, though; Bob Cerny had refused to transfer him out of Professor Shun's class, and he'd had to keep on seeing Libby around school. Between the two of them, plus the crazy bitch from U of SNY, those women had pretty much ruined his life.

Now all he had to look forward to was an Honor Board hearing — the investigation had taken most of the spring, and his defense counsel was encouraging him to plead and accept a "drop out of school and we won't tell anyone you cheated" deal before trial. As if. He still had to prove to Nana that he was worthy of her respect. He just hoped she'd give him a chance to do so.

Quinn Everly: Even a new pair of Kate Spade ballet flats couldn't put the spring back in Quinn's step. Quinn refused to believe that her 1L GPA was really a 1.73; she was having to fight automatic academic dismissal. In a last rally, she had written emails to Professor Shun, Dean Cerny, and anyone else who would listen saying that there must have been some mistake; she had done everything Law Stars said to do, including taking perfect notes and studying with smart people. Things couldn't actually have turned out this way.

What was she going to do now? Maybe she'd become a real star. She'd heard that *The Voice* was holding auditions in Newport next month. She thought she'd let her hair down, put on her shortest skirt, channel The Clash, and sing "I Fought the Law, and the Law Won."

Sarah Abernathy: It was probably a good thing that Connie was going away soon. Not that Sarah relished the idea of losing her best buddy to the rainforests of the Amazon, even temporarily. No, it was just that this spring had brought a certain call from the White House. About an opening on the bench. A high one. In Washington, D.C. And she wasn't allowed to tell a soul.

If she and Connie had even one long gabfest, Sarah would be in trouble. So better to wait until there was a formal ceremony in the Rose Garden. After that? She'd coax Connie down to D.C., and that fantastic student of hers, too.

Every Chief Justice of the United States needed a top advisor and several smarter-than-hell law clerks.

Bob Cerny: For Bob Cerny, the end of the school year was always liberating. But in the spring of 2015? He was thinking about taking on a ball and chain. After he sent out a "Congrats on finishing your 1L year" email, he headed to C & B to have a drink with his girlfriend of six months, Judge Sarah Abernathy. When last we heard from him, Dean Cerny was thinking about proposing. He had a feeling his true love was destined for great things, but, as the old song went, he might have to follow wherever his true love led.

Breyer Behl: Much to the aged goldfish's delight, at the end of the first year of law school (who'd ever thought they'd get through it?) came a move to a real tank with a stunningly renovated and enlarged courthouse, just like the real Supreme Court building. In the courtyard in the front? Lady Liberty, complete with the scales of justice (fish scales, in this case). He'd heard tell that more guy talk might be on its way; he was reserving judgment on this Matthews dude, though, until he met him in person.

Felix Frankfurter: Scruffy red wiener dogs belonged on brocade beds, not under airplane seats, and Felix had made sure that Connie got the message. He'd chewed right through that Coach doggie carrier she'd brought home, and he'd enjoyed it. Secretly, though, he was hoping for a trip to the badger fields of Bavaria, his ancestors' homeland. He could already feel the wind in his fur, the soft peat under his paws, and the tasty rodent in his mouth. Well, as long as Connie sprung for the Prada carrier instead, maybe being a traveling kind of dachshund wouldn't be so bad.

Angel Behl: Life on the road was amazing, but in the five years since Libby had gone off to college, it had gotten kind of lonely. During the spring of 2015, Angel was going to settle down for a few months, and Newport was as good a place as any to do it. In his suitcase? A pewter bracelet with dachshunds running around it, plus the fanciest leash and collar to be had in the Buenos Aires leather market. He could hardly wait to dig them out, give them to someone special, and let the summer get started. He was thinking that his writing needed to take a new turn. Maybe it was finally time to write his 9/11 story.

Ah, here they went . . . his plane was about to land in Providence. From there, it was only a short drive to Newport.

If loving Constance Tu Shun was wrong, Angel didn't want to be right.

Afterword

Libby Behl was not alone in losing her mother on September 11, 2001. The parents of more 3000 children died in the attacks, and eleven children whose fathers were killed that day were born in the months that followed.

Maria Behl was not a real person. Many accounts of 9/11, however, focus on the hundreds of brave men who helped at Ground Zero and neglect to mention that three female first responders were killed there. What's more, when the Twin Towers collapsed, many civilians — some undoubtedly women — were inside, trying to help others escape. While we may never know their names, we honor them just the same.

We will never forget.

Acknowledgments

Sincere thanks to:

Paula Beck, Clare Coleman, Debbie Dennis, Deborah Gordon, Caroline Leavitt, Abby McElroy, Justin Pidot, Jennifer Taub, Richard Tucker, Valerie Tucker, and Kim Ablon Whitney — for being patient and encouraging readers (sometimes over and over again).

Lee Carpenter — for the double puns.

Danny Markel — for supporting me from the first minute, even if our blog post didn't work as well as we thought it would. All through the first drafts of this novel, I chatted with you about it on Facebook. I am so sad that you were gone before you could read the final version. We carry you with us in our hearts.

Sarah Smith — for believing in my writing from the very beginning, long, long before anyone else did (including me). I've learned so much from you over the years; you're truly one of the greats.

Lisa Belkin, Lynn O'Rourke Hayes, Dahlia Lithwick — three wonderful friends, wonderful writers, wonderful supporters. Lisa told me that I definitely could write a novel — no problem (hah!). She told me to do it if I loved it and to stop stressing about all the rest. Lynn told me to do it in beautiful places. Dahlia? Well, they say that every protagonist has a little bit of the author in her; the Dahlia fan in Libby is all me.

Sarah Buttenwieser — for helping me think through what it would be like to grow up without a mom.

Mike Dorf — for the opportunity to explore some ideas on law and justice on Dorf on Law, setting up the possibility for Connie to work through them with her students.

Kevin Oates — the real Bob Cerny, so named because of the mystery sports jersey that ended up in the Oates household one day when Kevin was 17 years old. The fictional Bob Cerny only wishes he could be as great a Dean of Students as is Kevin.

About the Author

Lisa McElroy is a law professor, writer, wife, mom, and world traveler. Her two dachshunds and one French bulldog are not quite as demanding as Felix, but close. Lisa reads a book and bakes a loaf of bread almost every day. Her two daughters tolerate her reading and devour her bread. She has no idea how to make mini quiches.

Lisa has published eleven children's books, most of them about interesting and iconic Americans. Her essay for NPR's *This I Believe* was published in an anthology about parenthood; her reading of the essay was broadcast in the spring of 2013.

Lisa is a tenured Associate Professor of Law at Philadelphia's Drexel University Thomas R. Kline School of Law, where she teaches Family Law, a seminar on the United States Supreme Court, writing, and advocacy. For two Terms, she wrote the "Plain English" column for SCOTUSblog. She regularly provides commentary on the Supreme Court for NPR (Los Angeles, Portland, Philadelphia) and CBS Radio (Dallas/Ft. Worth). She has published op-eds in the *New York Times*, the *Washington Post*, the *National Law Journal*, the *Philadelphia Inquirer*, the *Houston Chronicle*, and several other papers and websites. She has been interviewed about the Supreme Court for the *New York Times*, the *Wall Street Journal*, the *National Law Journal*, *Slate*, *Salon*, *Modern Health Care*, the *Huffington Post*, and other publications.

Lisa is a travel expert who contributes to a wide variety of national publications, including AARP.com, *Huffington Post*, the *New York Times'* Motherlode, *Redbook*, *Kiwi*, *Parenting* (now defunct), *TravelAge West*, TravelingMamas, FamilyTravel.com, and Family Travel Network. Lisa has appeared on the *Today* show, CNN, the

Satellite Sisters, NPR, the *Gayle King Show*, and many other radio and television programs. She and her books have been featured and reviewed in the *Washington Post*, the *Chicago Tribune*, *Legal Times*, *People*, *Time*, *Parents*, NBC *Nightly News*, and other newspapers, magazines, and programs across the country.

An Interview with Lisa McElroy

What are your passions?

I am a Supreme Court junkie, and nothing tickles me more than when students, radio and TV producers, and random people off the street ask me questions about law and justice. Even though I live in Philadelphia, I am a proud member of the Red Sox Nation. I'm devastated that Michigan lost to Louisville in the 2013 NCAA finals. Nothing is more fun than standing in front of a class of students and talking about law. The best way to relax? Crawling under the covers with a dog or two and a really good book. Hanging out with my two adolescent daughters is the best, especially if we're talking about the Supreme Court, or the Red Sox, or our dogs, or what we're reading, or what's going on in their incredibly fascinating lives.

What's so exciting about the United States Supreme Court?

The majesty of the law never gets old. The fact that our Constitution has been around for over 200 years and has only been amended twenty-seven times speaks to consistency and fairness. "Equal Justice Under Law" inspires me to strive for justice. And the pizza in the Supreme Court cafeteria is darn good.

You seem like you're completely a dog fanatic.

My family is all about dogs. Maybe it's because my husband and I met walking our dogs in the park. Maybe it's because family dogs are just so vulnerable, so sweet, so grateful. Maybe it's because they bring so much love into our home.

What do you hope you'll see in your lifetime?

Cameras at the Supreme Court. Marriage equality for all (it happened!). Another Red Sox World Series. My older daughter's launch into space on the first Mars mission. My younger daughter's first gallery show. My great-grandchildren.

You're really into travel, just like Angel. Why?

I've gotten to attend a Samburu wedding in Kenya, hang out on the ocean floor with sea turtles in Belize, sail through the sky on a parasail with my younger daughter on Block Island, speak to Italian law students about how common law systems work in Genova. What's not to love?

Do you have a most memorable trip?

For my birthday a couple of years ago, my husband and I took a luxury white water rafting trip down the Futaleufu River in Patagonia, Chile. As if the Class V rapids weren't adventure enough, we got stuck in the biggest earthquake in fifty years. We were fine, but getting home was quite a challenge.

And you love traveling with the family, too? Why?

The whole family unwinds and hangs out together. There's usually no cell phone service. We eat a lot of crazy stuff (ice cream for breakfast, squid for dinner, anyone?). No one blow dries her hair. We explore together to find folk art to bring home — all the better to remember our trip. Only downside? Our dogs usually have to stay home.

What's next?

I'm working on the next novel about Libby, Connie, and Anderson. It's called *Life, Liberty, and the Pursuit of Happiness.*

Do you like to hear from readers?

Who doesn't? Check out my website at www.lisamcelroy.com and get in touch!

Visit us at *www.quidprobooks.com*.